"Where is God when I hurt?"

"Why doesn't He heal me?"

If you or someone you love suffers from pain, you know what it feels like to be

weary and ill from painkillers,

exhausted from an agony that won't go away,

frustrated over prayers that seem unanswered.

Jane Grayshon has experienced the suffering. For more than a decade following routine surgery, this vivacious nurse – and her loved ones – have fought an almost daily battle against searing pain, the result of recurring post-operative infection.

As you read her beautiful story, you'll feel you've met a new friend who has walked the pathway you're walking. A friend who cares.

And you'll discover, as Jane Grayshon did, that even when God doesn't take the pain away, He provides a pathway through it, paved with His precious love.

A pathway through pain.

A PATHWAY THROUGH *Pain*

Pressing On Despite
Chronic Pain and Suffering

JANE GRAYSHON

Here's Life Publishers

First Printing, August 1990

Published by
HERE'S LIFE PUBLISHERS, INC.
P. O. Box 1576
San Bernardino, CA 92402

© 1990, Jane Grayshon
Published by special arrangement with Kingsway
    Publications, Eastbourne, England.
All rights reserved.
Printed by Dickenson Press, Inc., Grand Rapids, Michigan.

Library of Congress Cataloging-in-Publication Data
Grayshon, Jane.
    A pathway through pain : pressing on despite chronic pain and suffering /
Jane Grayshon.
        p.   cm.
    ISBN 0-89840-291-3
    1. Grayshon, Jane—Health. 2. Intractable pain—Patients—Great Britain—
Biography. 3. Intractable pain—Religious aspects—Christianity. 4. Pregnan-
cy, Ectopic—Patients—Great Britain—Biography. I. Title.
    RB127.G73   1990
      616'.9472—dc20   90-4626
                                                        CIP

Unless designated otherwise, Scripture quotations are from *The Holy Bible: New International Version,* © 1973, 1978, 1984 by the International Bible Society. Published by Zondervan Bible Publishers, Grand Rapids, Michigan. Other Scripture references are taken from the Good News Bible (GNB).

Cover photography by Dennis Frates, Oregon Scenics.
Cover design by Cornerstone Graphics.

For More Information, Write:
L.I.F.E.—P.O. Box A399, Sydney South 2000, Australia
Campus Crusade for Christ of Canada—Box 300, Vancouver, B.C., V6C 2X3, Canada
Campus Crusade for Christ—Pearl Assurance House, 4 Temple Row, Birmingham, B2 5HG, England
Lay Institute for Evangelism—P.O. Box 8786, Auckland 3, New Zealand
Campus Crusade for Christ—P.O. Box 240, Raffles City Post Office, Singapore 9117
Great Commission Movement of Nigeria—P.O. Box 500, Jos, Plateau State Nigeria, West Africa
Campus Crusade for Christ International—Arrowhead Springs, San Bernardino, CA 92414, U.S.A.

*To all those
who are hurting somewhere inside*

Contents

Acknowledgments

There are many who have consciously helped me in the writing of this book. To them I would like to extend special thanks, especially to Jo Coates, Beth Harrison and Eric Wright, the love and sensitivity behind whose comments have shone in my darkness.

Many more people are unaware of how deeply their care is appreciated, or even of the fact that they have helped simply by being who they are, by suffering alongside me. I am thinking particularly of my husband, Matthew, and of our parents and close friends — those not mentioned in the book but whose quiet self-giving and private prayers have upheld me throughout both crises and everyday life.

But the person whose loving support I must acknowledge most of all is my Lord. He is the one whose help and love I fail so often to recognize, who is always patient with me even when I forget so often to thank Him. Thank You, Lord, for helping me write this book; even (You know my trepidation when I say this!) thank You for giving me what I have to write about — my share in Your sufferings.

Pain Is Like a Tide

*All your waves and breakers have swept over me
(Psalm 42:7, NIV).*

A few years ago, a friend of mine named Sadie wrote to me. She described how life was particularly bleak since she had developed a chronic illness which debilitated her and crippled the lifestyle of the whole family. I recognized so many of the feelings she described: her sorrow at seeing how she was affecting the children; her guilt and sense of failure that even her husband was forced to consider changing his job in order to cope better at home; her own feeling that she could not fight on much longer.

"I am struggling so much to come to terms with my illness," she wrote. "I end up with such doubts about healing, but I can't find anyone who fully understands. They could cope better with visiting a person in the hospital with a short-term illness, but something chronic is much harder to understand. What do you think?"

In this book I share some of my thoughts and feelings as I have tried to answer this question. I have focused on some specific times of intense pain and suffering in my own experience; times which I hope are representative of the ongoing struggles shared by Sadie and, no doubt, by countless others who are suffering long-term pain.

Having had my eyes opened to how much other people suffer in life (though in different ways from me), I have tried to be completely honest in describing the apparent contradictions which Christ has shown me. He has asked me to trust Him to the extent that I would accept pain, yet still maintain my expectation of His healing; to know comfort, yet still have many reasons to fear; to believe His promises, even in the midst of continued despair; to be aware of active victory, yet only through a passive submission to His will.

Although I have concentrated on my own pain, which is primarily physical, I hope this book will offer comfort and encouragement to all those who, like me, may have no obvious sign of suffering such as a wheelchair but who are hurting somewhere inside. Their pain may be caused by the unhappiness of a broken marriage; by bereavement of a dimension from which one cannot envision ever recovering; by knowing the burden of handicapped or difficult children; or by a life of fundamental aloneness in which the underlying stories may be diverse.

Pain is like a tide which comes and goes in waves of intensity. While writing, I have found myself fluctuating between the past and the present tense as the waves have continued to wash over me, then recede. My prayer is that in each person's awareness of his pain as he reads this book, the Lord will speak as clearly as He has spoken to me during my own painful recollections; that He may be a part of the suffering of each reader, even if He does not do what they most want and take the suffering away.

PART ONE

Overtaken
by Pain

1. My Soul Is Overwhelmed

My soul is overwhelmed
(Matthew 26:38).

Life with three brothers had many challenges. Keeping up with them became my determined goal from an early age.

It was very important to me that I learn to survive their masculine teases without being labeled a sissy. Stories of my grandmother and her eight brothers were a great encouragement to me: If she could survive eight brothers then I would make sure I could keep up with just three.

"*You* can't go up our rope ladder . . . "

"*You* can't climb to the top of the pear tree . . . "

Challenges such as these created from my earliest years a deep desire never to give others the opportunity to label me a weakling. And if they added, "'Cause you're a girl!" or "'Cause you're too young!", I would be all the more likely to rise to the challenge. I would take a huge breath and steel myself against any fear or pain in order to climb the disputed pear tree. On reaching the top I would feel exhilarated, in spite of my bleeding knees and the ribbons falling out of my pigtails.

I have memories of a wonderful childhood. From the very beginning my parents showed me that life is full, rich and fascinating. Endowed with a vivacious personality and coupled with strong determination, I have always loved rising to the challenges which life so generously offers. I have never been one to give up. I grew up believing that the exercise of willpower, coupled with a modicum of ingenuity, would carry me through to the solution of any problem. It does not come easily to me, therefore, to discover that there are situations with which I cannot cope.

I have had a rude awakening. Pain has become a prominent thread in the tapestry of my life and I have frequently been driven to the point of crying out in anguish, "I can't bear any more!"

It was during four dark months in 1980 that I came closest to giving up all together. I can never adequately describe the totality of my exhaustion with illness, with pain, with life itself.

In February, when the crisis began, I was already profoundly weary from a chronic low-level pain. Though I knew it was "normal" for me, I still winced every time I moved too vigorously and felt the heavy ache. Pain-killers were either not strong enough or they made me feel sick. Anyway, I tended not to take them as I feared that they would lose their effect if I took them too often. I dreaded having nothing to fall back on.

Pain began to be an unwelcome part of every conversation, so much that I would secretly think, *I hope this ends soon; I need to rest.* Yet I couldn't rest, for the pain made me restless. And if I were alone I would yearn for conversations, to distract me. Neither I nor my caring friends could win. There was no remedy. I easily became irritable, which in turn made me more irritable because I knew I was being short-tempered and hated myself for it.

On top of this situation, acute pain broke in. At first I thought I was pregnant. For two weeks my spirits rose, only to be dampened by the extra tiredness. As the pain increased, my excitement faded. My experience as a midwife told me that my symptoms were ominous.

Somehow I managed to keep working. As a registered nurse I cared for lots of patients who were complaining of pain, but inside I felt rather unsympathetic toward those who were obviously not genuine. I would catch a glimpse of them giggling with their boyfriends in the waiting room before they saw the doctor, when they would suddenly look very sorry for themselves and moan dramatically of "terrible pain, Doctor." I was often tempted to say,"You've no idea what terrible pain is if you can giggle through it." But I did not speak.

One of the doctors for whom I worked was Richard, my own doctor. I was not ready to talk about myself—least of all to him. I suppose I knew too well what he might find if he examined me. Still, I kept going. Every evening I would drive home along the foggy Midlands roads and just flop into bed. My husband Matthew was working so hard training for full-time ministry that he hardly noticed how much time I spent in bed. He ate his meals at the seminary, so he didn't realize that I wasn't cooking. He was so tired that he slept soundly through my fitful hours of trying to find a comfortable sleeping position.

On one particular Tuesday I was unable to walk briskly around the wards. I had to collect a blood sample for research from a patient in labor. While I was doing so, the other midwife with me was so comforting toward the patient that I found myself wishing I were on the receiving end of such comfort. Instead I tried simply to keep going, keep going . . .

In everything I did, I had to give myself instructions. *Keep walking down this corridor. You can do it.*

Walk over to pick up a syringe and needle. Force yourself. Walk over there. Keep upright.

Smile to that person. Make your eyes smile as well so he won't detect how much pain you're in.

The fighting part of my nature was determined not to give in. I hoped that if I ignored the pain it might all just resolve itself. If anyone had perceived the agony I was in and had asked me about it, I would have crumpled. In one way I longed for my pain to be noticed — yet at the same time I was terrified of what that might mean.

On Wednesday I had to help with some medical students' exams. Normally I loved that, for I mercilessly teased all the doctors and professors who conducted the exams. I liked to pull them down a peg or two from the pompous stance they all assumed to terrify the medical students. They, in turn, were so bored with examining that they enjoyed a bit of banter. I had quite a reputation for being fun.

That Wednesday, though, I was very subdued. There was none of the usual dramatics and singing, and at the end of the morning session Richard asked me about it.

"You all right?" he asked quietly as we walked across an enclosed bridge for lunch. The door at the end was open, revealing tables laden with delicious food and girls in starched white hats ready to serve us generously. I thought I might vomit just at the sight of it.

"Not bad," I replied, carefully averting my eyes from him lest he read the truth.

Richard looked at me incredulously and for the first time I dared to meet his gaze. "I think perhaps I need some antibiotics."

There. I'd said it. Surely I could be pleased with myself. I also could tell Matthew later that I had "confessed," and he would be pleased and relieved. A few antibiotics would clear everything up, wouldn't they?

Richard looked at me questioningly for a minute, then agreed.

"Okay. Get a prescription pad and I'll sign it."

I slipped quietly out of the room. By now my abdomen felt as if it were on fire. I knew I should not have tried to appear so calm and composed in front of Richard. I should have asked him at a more appropriate time when he could have examined me properly. He always trusted me to ask, and this time I had deliberately made it difficult for him. I was afraid.

Never mind, I consoled myself. *The antibiotics will soon work.*

The afternoon passed. I longed to lie down or even lean over a table and rest my head and my tummy.

I took the prescription to Richard, and after he signed it he looked up.

"You shouldn't be here. Get home and start chewing these." He added a request for a huge bottle of strong pain-killers.

"You won't take these all at once, will you?" He laughed heartily at his joke. I forced a weak smile. I could not laugh, because even the muscular movement of laughter caused the pain to sear through me. Perhaps it wasn't such a joke.

I did not go straight home. I went to my sister's office and wrote up all the outstanding reports, dealt with all correspondence and tidied up my files. I didn't want to leave until I knew everything was in order and up to date. I must have sensed that I would not be there again for a long time.

I spent the following days in bed. Matthew's face became more and more anxious, though he always tried to cheer me up whenever he brought me food and beverages. Every time he had to remove a tray of food I hadn't managed to eat, his face set a little more. He knew I was getting worse, but neither of us wanted to be the first to say so.

Two or three times we had to call the local doctor to see me. Once was on Saturday evening and the doctor seemed so hard pressed we almost felt he resented having to come out to see me at all.

"What can I do for you?" he asked curtly, getting out his prescription pad and flicking his pen, ready to write.

Matthew replied quickly, trying to save me from using my little energy on making explanations all over again. "Well, four years ago she had her appendix out and since then . . . ," he began.

"I am asking, what is the problem *now*?" The doctor twisted his pen impatiently, waiting to write.

I began to feel agitated. How could we avoid putting my present symptoms into the context of the last few years? This was no isolated dose of flu. I had not been completely healthy for the previous four years, ever since an undiagnosed abscess had burst a few weeks after a normal appendix operation in Edinburgh. It had poured its offensive, bug-ridden contents diffusely into my abdomen. Despite rigorous treatment by both surgery and antibiotics, the resultant highly-infectious micro-organisms had never been completely eradicated, though they hadn't caused me any problems for long periods of time. Yet every so often the inflammation reared its ugly head, each time bringing with it further debilitating illness and the possibility of grave consequences.

How could I summarize all that in one defensive sentence?

I was thankful to Matthew for acting as spokesman for me, because he still looked very calm. At the same time, he didn't understand medical terminology and I wondered if I shouldn't step in with some jargon to make the doctor stop and think more wisely. I decided I must if we were to be helped at all.

"I've had pelvic inflammatory disease ever since, with acute bouts of peritonitis intermittently. It seems to have flared up again now. I'm very sore."

"Any pyrexia?"

"No, but my temperature hardly ever goes up even when I have a bad bout. We don't understand why it doesn't."

The doctor had stopped listening as soon as I said no and was back to poising his pen over the prescription pad.

"No pyrexia. Well then, there's nothing seriously wrong. But I could give you some antibiotics if you really want some." He seemed pleased to be able to write something at last.

I looked helplessly toward Matthew. He often goes quiet when there's lots to say, as if he'll say nothing until he has sorted out all the thoughts that are clamoring in his mind. He stood thoughtfully, then his eyes met mine. I could see that he felt unable to argue against that great barrier, the "medical profession." It annoyed me once again that doctors can set themselves up as if their opinions must not be disputed.

Fortunately, I was not left without an argument. "Thank you for the prescription, but actually I've been on antibiotics since Wednesday."

"Oh?" He was caught slightly off guard, at least. "Well, they should be doing the trick."

"But they aren't, and it's three and a half days now. I'm getting worse, not better. And I feel so nauseated I can hardly take them."

He snapped his smart doctor's bag shut, lifted it off his knees and placed it on the floor. "I'd better have a look at your tummy then. Where is the pain?"

I pointed to the area over one side, carefully avoiding touching it because it was so tender. He laid his cold hand on the opposite side and gradually worked his way across my abdomen, pressing as if he were securing postage stamps rather than palpating me gently. I pulled my legs up involuntarily and drew a deep breath.

Matthew jumped to my defense. "Do be gentle. She's been through a lot," he pleaded quietly.

"This must be done," was the short reply.

When he finished, my hands were white from clenching my fists. I could not discuss things objectively now. Nausea swept over me in great waves but I was too shy to lean over the bowl in front of someone who made me feel so discomforted. It would serve him right if I were sick on him, I thought uncharitably. But then the pain seared through me once again, round to my back and to the tops of my legs. I closed my eyes to try to cope.

"I will change the prescription for different antibiotics." The doctor picked up that wretched pad and pen once again. "If there's no improvement by Monday, see your own G.P."

I opened my eyes a little. Matthew seemed vaguely relieved. He must have thought this remedy was worth some respect. I could not share his confidence but for his sake I would do as I was told. In any case, what alternative did I have?

I mustered the energy to ask about what was bothering me. "I feel so sick, I don't know that I can keep the antibiotics or the pain-killers down. I must have something . . . " I looked at him pleadingly.

"Here, take this." The doctor rummaged in his black bag once again.

"What is it?" I never gave my patients any medication without explaining what it was or how it worked, and I didn't intend to accept anything without knowing about it.

"Just take it." He held it out to me and nodded firmly before mumbling, "You nurses are all the same." His hardened eyes looked past me with little compassion and inside myself I shriveled up. I was too weary to refuse. I took it.

After he had gone, everything became a blur. The mysterious pill made my head swim and it was hard for me to distinguish between what was real and what was only in my mind. My thoughts drifted around, accompanied by the fast throb of my heartbeat, almost like swirling music with a pounding drum in the background.

Matthew came and went, kneeling beside my bed and speaking softly and gently. His care soothed me very much. I was so grateful, it was little cost for me to force myself to smile at him. But whenever I closed my eyes I was back in a world of pain. Sometimes I had nasty hallucinations, sometimes I sat bolt upright in bed or leaned over to try to shift the pain. Always I was aware of the pain.

On Monday morning, neither Matthew nor I had any doubt as to what we should do. After a quick phone call to an understanding secretary in the department where I worked, I had an appointment to see Richard the same day.

I do not know quite how I got myself together enough to reach the doctor's office. Matthew drove me there, taking immense care to avoid bumps in the road so as not to jolt my aching body. I refused his arm up the few stairs. Once again my age-old fear of being labeled a "sissy" was taunting me. I mustn't be weak. It was hard and I had to cling to the bannister for support but I made it independently.

As Matthew held open the door of the department, my absolute terror of what Richard might decide about me was temporarily put to one side. Every thought I had was focused on keeping going.

Once again I programmed myself. *Walk, Jane. Just get to that chair there and lean on that. Keep your body upright or they'll see you and think you're doing a dramatic mimic of a patient in pain. Don't give them the opportunity to think you're a fraud. Instead, make yourself look normal. Don't stoop with the pain . . .*

I tormented myself with thoughts that I may be taken as a fraud. I think this was because I so detested being treated as one in Edinburgh when I first became ill in 1976. I dread the idea of being ignored because I do not seem genuine. And yet when the pain is severe, I crave most of all the genuineness of somebody's care. So I force myself to look as normal as possible and try to keep from showing any signs of pain, so that only a genuinely caring person can perceive how I am underneath.

I heard Richard's distinctive step. He beamed at us cheerfully. I swallowed hard and let go of Matthew's hand, wondering what else I was letting go of in the process — my fighting, my pretending that all was better than it was.

"See you down in the room," Richard called to me as he whisked into the secretary's office to pick up my chart. He soon caught up with me. My progress was slow, every step an act of will. I wished that I did not have to walk with him beside me.

I thought I saw him glance down at my hand when I grasped involuntarily at my abdomen while taking a step which reverberated through me. He would be getting suspicious. Had he also noticed how distracted I was? Would he guess why?

The corridor seemed endless, but at last I was in the examination room. With relief I almost fell into the black plastic chair to which Richard had gestured. I could not relax, though, lest my face accidentally reveal the contortion which I felt inside.

I was still so afraid he would think I was a coward. I wanted to show my composure. I worked for the man — I didn't want to give him reason to stop respecting me.

I answered Richard's questions very briefly, for even the effort of speaking increased my discomfort; but I was honest. After scribbling a few notes, Richard leaned over to take my pulse. There was silence as he counted.

He fiddled with his new digital watch, his face puzzled. *Has he still not worked out how to use it?* I wondered. I would frequently tease him that it was maybe too complicated for him, but today there was none of our usual light-hearted banter. I closed my eyes, sensing that I was beginning to take on the passive role of a patient. I felt I was being forced to "give in," even if that made me more vulnerable. I couldn't overcome the pain by fighting it or by ignoring it. It had overcome me.

"A hundred and thirty-six?" The surprise in Richard's voice was mixed with obvious concern. I was so accustomed to fighting for a doctor to take my condition seriously that I now didn't quite know what to say.

But Richard was not waiting for me to reply; he was counting once again.

"Your pulse is 136, Jane." His face, normally rather mischievous with his dark moustache and dimples, was quite neutral. "Bit high, isn't it?" His endeavors to remain unperturbed in front of me were countered by my seeing his pen circling my pulse rate strongly on my case notes. "I'd better examine you."

I got onto the couch, raising my legs slowly to avoid jarring my abdomen. I realized it was no use pretending any longer. I could have wept—but not just from the pain. My mind was totally confused. I didn't know whether to be relieved that at last I was being seen as I really was, or to be afraid of the seriousness of my situation. Physical pain and emotional distress form a potent and destructive partnership.

After he had finished, Richard straightened his arms and leaned the palms of his hands on the couch.

"You know what this means, don't you?" It was more of a statement than a question. I opened my mouth to speak, but my voice wouldn't work.

2. Let This Cup Pass From Me

*Father, if it is possible,
may this cup be taken from me
(Matthew 26:39).*

"I'll book surgery for you for 7 P.M. but I'll make sure the ward is ready to receive you immediately."

I looked at the wall clock. It was 5 P.M.

Richard shuffled slightly. He knew me well enough to come straight to the point instead of waffling around a subject—and he also knew that given half a chance I would question and dispute everything.

"Hang on!" I cleared my throat. I could see he was resolute, but my mind was still full of questions. "What do you think it is?"

"Maybe an ectopic. You have all the signs."

I gazed at the wall. So . . . maybe I had been pregnant after all, but the baby was in my fallopian tube. For some reason I did not feel sorry for this baby as I did when I nursed other women with ectopics. Instead, I was full of regret that I hadn't enjoyed all the glee of a first pregnancy.

Matthew would have been delighted, and so very proud of me. I would have borne my parents' first grand-child—and I their only daughter among three sons. They would have been thrilled: my mother because she and I could have enjoyed the unique relationship of a mother and her expectant daughter, and my father in a different way because I was, in his own words, his "darling daughter." And I would have loved the pregnancy. I'd have made sure I always looked fresh and pretty, relishing this time of being eminently female.

These thoughts flashed across my mind within seconds. All this had suddenly become impossible. The implications were far reaching. The previous June, during another emergency crisis, Richard had had to remove one ovary and fallopian tube. If this was an ectopic pregnancy now, it was in my only remaining fallopian tube. Once this other side was removed, as Richard would possibly do in two hours, then I would no longer be able to have a baby. I was not only saying goodbye to my first, but also to my only possible pregnancy.

I turned my mind away from such an idea. "What if it's not an ectopic?" My voice lacked my usual vivacity.

"Then I'll have to open you up to see what it is." Richard was certainly not going to budge an inch. "See you in surgery," he said firmly.

Back in the ward I could not avoid being seen by others on the staff—my friends. Even with the supposed "security" of being taken seriously by Richard, I still could not allow myself to trust them enough to indicate that I was in great pain. In two hours I might be found to have nothing much wrong, in which case they would know I had been complaining about nothing. Only sissies did that.

Rather than risk such a horrifying label, I put on my act yet again, looking cheerful and saying airily, "Oh! I'm off for another operation, folks. Unzipping me again!" And they laughed, as my words suggested they should. But inside I begged them to break through my role-playing, to sit down beside me and weep with me.

Matthew was quiet as he escorted me to the ward. When faced with a number of possible outcomes to any problem he never speculates, "If it's this, then this will happen." He waits until it has happened. Thus he did not comment on anything, but he kept me going with his quiet sympathy and love. He was well practiced at the whole ritual of my illness, hospitalization and surgery. He had seen me through it so many times before.

They were kind enough to me on the ward, but I felt impatient at being subjected to unnecessary questions. Partly, I was bored at recounting the history of my illness and partly I longed to escape from the intensity of physical suffering. Having to repeat it gave me less time alone to compose myself and — I suppose — to pray.

"You don't need to ask me that. It's all in my chart," I sighed to a junior nurse at last. She slipped out of my room, biting her lip. Poor girl. A nurse was probably a daunting enough prospect for her to care for, without my putting her down like that.

Once I had been prepared for surgery, I valued my short time alone before 7 P.M. I wasn't praying in a formal way; just thinking in front of God. I knew He was with me, though now, as so often, I couldn't feel Him. I kept placing myself in His hands, asking Him to help me accept how I was. So much putting on a brave face in front of others makes it difficult for me to understand exactly how I am, even within myself.

Very soon, it seemed, I was being roused from the anesthetic. I recognized the sensations because of previous operations: the thud as I was lifted from the trolley and dumped back in bed; the inability to cough without pain piercing through me; the helplessness.

Then I became aware of someone beside me.

"Can you hear me, Jane?" It was Richard's voice. I grunted and flickered my eyes, but they were too heavy to stay open.

"How do you feel?" He was very kind.

"Fine, thanks." I croaked my usual evasive reply. He would know how I felt; there was no need for me to launch into a moan.

"Well, I — er — thought I'd pop in to see you, to tell you about it."

"What did you find?" Such a long sentence required me to take a big breath at the end, and I regretted it. Big breaths hurt.

"It — er — it wasn't too good, actually." Richard sounded quite tense. "Sometimes with an acute infection you get fluid accumulation in the fallopian tube; and sometimes there's a little pus. But — er — you had frank pus. And it wasn't neatly contained in your tube. It was all over your pelvis."

I swallowed. There was a pause.

"I knew you'd find it hard to believe so I tried to take a picture." He knew my hang-ups all right. "Unfortunately the camera wouldn't work — it was broken. You'll just have to take my word for it."

The impact of his words hadn't sunk in yet. Then he added, "I'm giving you constant intravenous antibiotics for five days." I knew that putting them directly into my bloodstream was a much more rigorous way of dealing with the infection than giving me pills which I'd been taking since Wednesday.

For the first time I began to realize that Richard was treating this very seriously. Perhaps I could stop being so fearful that I was a fraud and begin to trust what I was being told.

Richard was still hovering beside me. He was quiet, uneasy, solemn. I rarely saw him like this—only occasionally when he was grieved at seeing a young patient with cancer. He loathed being unable to cure people.

"I think I'd better call Matthew to tell him." He sounded a bit happier now that he'd thought of something positive to do. He paused. "You both know that he can come in and see you any time."

This final comment before he walked slowly away to the telephone was the one which made me sense the seriousness of my condition. To be allowed to visit someone in the hospital at any time was a privilege reserved for relatives of people who were really ill—not for those just recovering from operations, and certainly not for frauds. I was very slow in allowing the facts to sink in, but at last it began to dawn on me that I really was very ill.

The trouble was—and still is—that my fear of being labeled a sissy was so strong that I fought against and denied the fact that I was in pain. I told myself that however rotten I felt, I must not trust feelings. I was so accustomed to pushing to the back of my mind any question that I could in fact be in pain, that I took a long time to believe it. Richard and Matthew had to repeat over and over to me how ill I actually was before I could believe that complaining of pain does not necessarily mean I am a fraud.

And once I did begin to believe it, I actually became excited. It seemed wonderful to imagine that others did not think I had been moaning and moping about nothing. I felt a certain amount of glee and, I suppose, pride, that I had achieved one aim in life—that of being brave, of keeping my chin up.

Matthew's visit gave me even more reason to feel vindicated. It must have been odd to him that I should be so psychologically elated when, physically, I was very low. I was lying still in the bed when he came, and for a change I was passive. I hardly opened my eyes, nor spoke. He stroked my hand gently.

"Richard called me last night, you know." Matthew said steadily.

I nodded. "He said he was going to."

"He said he didn't know how you managed to climb the stairs and walk into the office yesterday when you went to see him." I smiled. "He was bewildered. He said, 'If it had been you or me, Matthew, we'd only have gotten there by being carried in on a stretcher!'"

My chest glowed with pride. Perhaps I felt just as I used to many years before, when I proved to my brothers that I could do brave or precarious things like climbing the pear tree to the very top.

Matthew continued, "He also told me of his resolve never again to believe your face when you're unwell. You look so cheerful and you put so much effort into appearing normal that you make it very hard for anyone to realize how bad you may be feeling inside."

I smiled again, appreciating Matthew's understanding. When I opened my eyes I saw his face furrow as he spoke again. "I'm glad he seems to have you figured out at last. But . . . " and he held my hand more tightly. He was troubled. "My dear Jane. He's obviously concerned about you. He said you're seriously ill." His voice trailed away.

I was quiet for a bit. "I know," was all I could say. Psychologically I was buoyant with my new-found freedom in not feeling condemned as a fraud, yet physically I remained far from well.

The five days of intravenous drugs passed slowly. Time was measured according to the constant drip, drip, drip of my intravenous infusion. Yet even this high dose of two different antibiotics did not bring the dramatic improvement everybody had expected. The February days stretched into a week, and even a month. March turned to April. Easter approached and I was still lying in the same bed in the hospital. I may have looked the same, but all the while I was getting weaker.

I became increasingly passive. I had to be encouraged and helped to sit up, because I had little enthusiasm left to get out of bed and prove that I was trying hard to make progress. I had to be cajoled into eating food. The nurses had to pour my drinks and pass them to me in order to maintain my fluid intake. I had to be offered bedpans instead of my actively asking for them. I could neither muster the physical energy to hold a book nor the concentration to read it. I simply looked forward to the brief release brought to me by the pain-killing drugs, but even that respite was tainted by the dread of the side-effects.

My spirits sank as well. Though I was never one to give up easily, there was no fight left in me. Two or three times Richard let me go home for a few days, to see if that would help lift my morale and bring back my normal drive to live. Each time I had to be re-admitted within a week or so for pain-killing and anti-sickness injections. Medically, there was very little else that could be done for me. I had been pumped full of drugs and vitamins, yet I remained pale, listless, uninterested, ill and in pain—more pain, I feared, than I would be able to bear. Always I was in pain.

On one of my spells out of the hospital, I stayed in the home of one of Matthew's college professors, Tina. In the hospital I had yearned to be nearer Matthew and I also wanted to be within the deeply caring fellowship of his seminary.

There was a group of people who had joined together to pray every Monday since I had been admitted to the hospital in February. They and others had also reached out to me by visiting me, or by writing to me, or by sending thoughtful messages via Matthew. God's love was clearly seen among so many people in the seminary, and I wanted to drink in as much of it as possible. The atmosphere was quite different from the hospital. With persuasion, Richard had conceded that I could be discharged into Tina's care.

Poor Tina. I don't think she knew what she was getting into. For me, my time in her home was like a spiritual oasis where I could drink in her comfort and love. But in every other way, I sank lower and lower.

By being nearer to one another, Matthew and I could see more clearly how far from my normal self I was. In Tina's flat, we were both confronted by the extent to which my pain imposed itself on our relationship. We could not enjoy quiet, intimate conversations because the unspoken tension of my illness prevented us from being totally relaxed; and of course any physical expression of our relationship was completely thwarted.

I began to wonder if Matthew ever considered how much better off he would be if he had married someone else. I asked him what he would do if I should die. Every time I asked, he talked of returning to Sarawak where he had once taught. We both knew that he would never be able to fulfill this desire with me, because of my medical history.

The seed of doubt was sown in my mind. Would it not be to Matthew's benefit if I were to die? Of course he would mourn, he would grieve – but he would get over that. Would he not ultimately be more free if he were not burdened by me living in pain?

Throughout my sleepless nights I pondered the burden I was on others. My conclusion was always the same. However hard I had tried to make the gift of my life outweigh the burden of it, I was failing. I was certain that I was more burden than gift.

Even apart from Matthew I thought of the burden I was on Tina, on others having to visit me. I could not perceive that they themselves might be learning through the witness of my life.

I was all burden—even to myself. I had struggled on for so long, but eventually I became weary and sick of life itself. Finally, one day, I gave up hope.

It happened because of a telephone call to the hospital seeking help. I had to tell Richard I was unable to tolerate the dreadful pain any longer. I was unable to speak to Richard but another nurse, Pat, listened very understandingly. She took my message and promised to phone me back.

The silence in Tina's flat was suddenly broken by Pat's return phone call. I struggled to crawl over and answer it.

"Jane?" Pat spoke very gently.

"Yes, hi." I put on my jovial voice. "What did Richard say?"

"He said, 'Keep going.' "

"But, Pat, I phoned because I've run out of resources to be able to."

"Well, he said that when or if things get as bad as they were in February then you must come back to him."

I wondered how I could explain myself more clearly. "Things *are* as bad as they were in February. In fact, I feel worse. I've no strength left with which to fight now."

"You're that bad, Jane?" Pat wanted to be sure she had the message right. "Remember how seriously ill you were then."

I remembered all right. "Pat, I'm desperate."

"Hang on. I'll phone you right back."

I knew that each time she went, she must be interrupting Richard between patients at his busy Wednesday morning clinic. Normally, I would have been helping him. I knew he hated interruptions. She must have been very diplomatic.

I knelt on the floor of Tina's hall, leaning over the low table while I waited the second time. I could not face the tedium of making my way clumsily to a comfortable chair. No chair was comfortable in any case—no chair, nor bed, nor any position. I could not escape.

Pat did not take long. This time her voice, though still gentle, was strained.

"I've spoken to Richard and explained more fully how you are." She hesitated. "He said that you must be assured you can come to the hospital at any time, day or night, for adequate pain relief."

I could not believe my ears. I was being given the instructions we give to terminal patients. This was what we said to patients when we could not cure them.

There was no emotion in my voice when I spoke. "Was there nothing else he said? Can't he do anything else, Pat?"

Pat was obviously choosing her words carefully. "He said there is nothing more positive he can do." Then she added, "He felt very helpless and very sorry for you."

I replaced the receiver. So that was it then. I made my way to the living room. My mind was completely vacant, numb, except for the words: *Nothing more he can do . . . nothing more he can do.*

I do not recall how many people I stared through as the day progressed. It was as if I had been given an anaesthetic which numbed me completely, though I was not asleep.

One visit I do remember, though. Matthew was with me when Colin, the president of the seminary, came. He seemed a shy man with little time for small talk in his busy life, but he had been wonderful throughout my illness, visiting me frequently in the hospital. I was very grateful, though I stood enough in awe of him to fear that, were I to share my deepest reactions, he might find them rather trite.

Colin asked me how I felt. My answer was, I thought, suitably objective. I avoided telling him how I felt emotionally, and chose rather to give him factual information. I told him of my phone call that morning.

Colin sat for a long time, keeping his gaze on me all the time until at last he asked, "Does this mean death, Jane?"

I was startled.

"Pardon?" I tried to create time in which to consider the full implications of this unexpected question. I was not used to talking intimately with Colin and he was pretty near the bone now. I was terrified I might cry — courageous me, in front of Colin to whom I did not wish to appear a weepy woman. And what would Matthew think? I was acutely embarrassed that he was there, listening. How did Colin dare to be so direct as this?

By the time he had repeated his question, I knew he expected an answer from me. I looked at Matthew. With relief I saw he was not surprised by Colin. I tried to follow his example and keep calm.

"I suppose it does . . . yes."

Colin stayed with us, counseled us, prayed with us. I will never forget his help. He had forced me to face the most important question. He enabled me to answer it — and with Matthew.

But that afternoon, something snapped. Suddenly I could not go through any more. God was asking too much of me.

My thoughts of how much of a burden I was to others grew as they merged with the idea that my body was too much of a burden to me. There was nothing more to be done, and Richard was very sorry. With Colin's help, Matthew and I had joined hands and faced my death together. Now I could not bear to wait.

This was my Gethsemane. I was facing death some time soon. The suffering while I waited was more than I could bear. It was too much to ask of me. I had that huge bottle of pills which Richard had prescribed in February with his "joke" about not taking them all at once. Wouldn't it help me and Matthew and Tina and Colin and all those in seminary if I just speeded things up? Wouldn't that give a nice happy ending instead of my having to bear this seemingly endless pain?

"Tina!" I cried at the top of my voice in the middle of the night when temptation became unbearable. And to God I cried in a whisper, "Let this cup pass from me . . . "

3. *Not My Will, but Thine*

*Yet not My will, but Thine
(Luke 22:42).*

I had come to the end of my rope, and in so doing I had discovered that "fighting" was not an answer to the problem of personal pain. There came a point at which my determined spirit was no longer my ally. I had to come to terms with the fact that there is a mystery about suffering, and I had to begin to plumb that mystery, its depths.

"I mustn't, must I?" But even in the depths of my anguish, there was in me some stirring of affirmation that God's will should be done, not mine.

When she heard my desperate call, Tina rushed to me, her curlers clinging resolutely to the ends of her hair. Her ample bosom heaved as her eyes focused to take in the scene: a bucket beside my bed in case an overdose made me vomit; a towel laid neatly across the sheet lest I made a mess, and me clutching the bottle of pain pills.

Quickly she moved forward to kneel beside the bed, taking both my hands in hers.

"Have you taken any?" Her voice was earnest. She realized immediately the implications of what she saw.

I shook my head.

I could not speak now. Words seemed trite, inadequate; too shallow to describe the depths I felt. It was as if my experience of suffering had led me to a window beyond which there lay a whole new world. The world on which I was gazing that night was the mystery of suffering.

As Tina knelt beside me, the silent bond between us began to infuse warmth into my numbness against life. If I felt nothing else, I was at least glad I was not alone while my eyes were opened to see that huge mysterious world. I suspect that she, too, saw the same picture as I.

Eventually I spoke. "God is just asking too much of me."

The compassion in Tina's eyes did not fade. With relief, I realized that she was not judging me. Indeed, she seemed to understand my pain and fears so completely that she knew I did not want an answer. The window through which we were both looking pointed to the infinite, the unanswerable. To have imagined we could give an answer with our finite minds would have been to deny what we were seeing.

"How can He allow this pain to go on so long? How can I express to Him that this is too much?" Tears began to flow down my cheeks — tears of anguish but also of relief that I was not being rejected even when hurling such strong questions into the air.

Slowly, very gently, Tina began to speak. Her voice was soft, almost a whisper. "I don't know," came her gentle reply. She knew I was not really asking her; I was shouting at God. I was trying to demand that He explain Himself to me.

She must have known she would have squashed me if she had sounded strong in the face of my weakness. She was aware that we were both at the mercy of God and wherever He chose to lead us. She was not proud that she had not been led to the same place as me; she knew the same could have been true for her had God so desired.

"I don't understand Him," she said softly. "He does seem to ask an awful lot of some people sometimes." She looked at her hands as her voice trailed away. She had obviously reminded herself of a time when God had seemed harsh to her.

There was a silence between us. I could see that it was hard for Tina to struggle with the memory of her pain, whatever had caused it. But her gentleness with me showed she had reached a point of acceptance, even though that point has to be reached again and again each time one relives the pain in one's mind. In these moments of loving sympathy Tina, almost unwittingly, was leading me toward a most important and health-giving insight. I — a fighter by nature — began to see that God wanted to give me the strength not to fight against His will but to embrace it. I thus began to understand one of the essential secrets within the mystery of suffering.

I lay back against the pillows for the first time that night. Slowly the tension I had felt began to ease as Tina's compassion washed over me. As her story unfolded, I realized that she was not surprised that I was at the end of my rope. She had been in that place herself. It was good for me to be taken into the heart of someone else's suffering. This was true compassion: She was able to share the burden of my pain because she recognized it. Because she had refused to run away from the hard questions within herself, she could also face them in me.

It was not Tina's story which was so moving, but the manner in which she talked. More clearly than any words, her quietness and calmness spoke of her complete acceptance of me in my despair. She was offering me the same acceptance which she had found for herself. She knew she would never completely understand God's wisdom. She had therefore allowed some questions to remain. She accepted the mystery of suffering.

The more I listened, the more encouraged I felt. Not that I was pleased that she had suffered so much; nor was there any special comfort in knowing that I was not the only person ever to experience Gethsemane. The source of my encouragement was the realization that I was not being dreadfully un-Christian for feeling as I did. If Tina had been taken to similar depths and desperation, and her story caused me to admire her all the more for it, then maybe I should not condemn myself.

I suddenly realized that probably many people have suffered similarly, but they have not dared to talk about it for fear that an intimately personal experience would be explained away glibly by someone who could not understand.

Before leaving me to rest for the last few hours of the night, Tina prayed with me. She did not impose any pious-sounding prayers. She spoke slowly, even haltingly, for she respected the very personal area between me and God where she knew she was treading.

In quietness and stillness she sought God's will with me. She asked that if, as it seemed, God was not going to rescue me from the suffering, I might know Him *in* it. Her prayer could not have been more appropriate. This was one of the times in life when to struggle to escape suffering was to lose touch with God. To accept it was to find His presence, that loving presence who never leaves us or forsakes us even in the harsh reality of pain.

The following day dawned bright and sunny. The sky was clear and blue, the spring air fresh. While I waited for Matthew to drop in on his way to morning worship, I was amazed to find myself enjoying watching the birds in the trees outside. They were not fighting their way through life. They just got on with it, busily content with everyday things. They chirped and sang; they flitted across to a different branch for a change of scene; they looked for worms on the lawn; they flew high up, carefree. They were not questioning how they would live. When difficulties arose they would either overcome them or they would die. They were not overburdened about that. Perhaps I should learn from them.

My musings were interrupted by the welcome click of the door. Matthew did not know, at first, why I clung to him so fervently when I saw him. In holding him as I did, I was showing my intent to hold on to life in this world.

Gradually I dared to give him hints of what had happened. His understanding response enabled me to unfold the full story of my temptation.

He skipped his first lecture in order to prolong our blessed time together, silently affirming his allegiance to me. The comfort Matthew gave me—and which my friends later brought me—was a lifeline. How much I needed the love and absence of condemnation they expressed to me! For years I had felt that I was unable to bear more, though in practice I had no option.

The reassurance and the acceptance I received brought courage. Strengthened by that, I experienced some sort of breakthrough. From this time onward I began to grow deeper and deeper into an acceptance of God's will for me, however hard it was to be.

Other people noticed and remarked upon the spirit of peace which welled up from deep within me, although I was still critically ill. As my week in Tina's home drew to an end, the seminary closed for Easter. I very much wanted to go to the final Thursday evening communion. I wanted to be among so many very caring Christians who had supported me in prayer through the long months.

It was a struggle to go the few yards from Tina's college flat to the chapel, but I wanted to make the effort. I remember feeling so weak that a friend had to help dress me. Once outside, I leaned my weak body against a supportive arm. Almost every step was an act of will:

Just get yourself to that handrail. Walk. Keep going. Rest your weight on that door handle for a minute, then walk again. Get to the next door before stopping again. Force yourself. Don't lose your momentum.

I recall one door being opened for me by someone who knew how ill I was but who had not visited me. As I walked through the door, his face suddenly froze. I still chuckle to myself as I picture him literally jumping to attention with a click of his heels. He almost saluted. If he had not been quite so frightened by his close proximity to death (in my person) I would have said what I was thinking, "Don't worry, I'm not in my coffin yet!"

The chapel doors were open when I approached and I could hear the welcoming hum of conversation before the service began. It had been two months since I attended a service, and my spirits rose excitedly. Although it was only forty-eight hours since that terrible night with Tina, now as I neared the chapel I knew that God had given me a new peace. Assuredly, this peace passes all human understanding — for, humanly speaking, nothing had changed. I had no reason to be peaceful, no hope of cure, no magic pills to relieve the pain and nausea. Yet I was filled right up to the top with God's peace.

A student whom I did not know handed me a hymn book. My heart and soul were so full with God's peace that I also felt joy, and the radiance of this joy merged into an enormous love toward everyone. It was as though I were discovering some new and wonderful gift from my Lord at every turn.

This joy, which had emerged from the deep peace, was the joy of accepting God's way for me. I had reached the point of conceding even subconsciously, "Lord, Your will be done, not mine."

Acceptance was not a passive submission to what I could not change. I had not *resigned* myself to God's will. I had done something much more positive than that. I had begun to *embrace* God's will, and as a result I discovered that some precious fruit was growing even within my suffering. Indeed, it grew from the very root of acceptance which Tina had offered to me.

The following two months were a hard test of this acceptance. Nothing changed dramatically. The pain was just as constant, just as intense. It was as if God were holding the whole situation before me and asking, "Will you accept My will, Jane? Or are you merely accepting My will because you hope that will bring about a change in the situation? For how long will you endure for My sake? As long as I desire, or until you run out of patience?"

But my trust in my Lord did not flag again. Indeed, as the weeks of April and May passed, my acceptance of His will grew.

During this lull in the storm, while I became no better but no worse either, Caroline, one of our prayer group, heard me make a tongue-in-cheek comment that only the sunshine in the Bahamas would do me any good. A seed was sown in her mind.

There were about ten couples who had committed themselves to prayer each week, all students on meager grants. Yet their desire was to be open to what God wanted. They were willing to do anything practical to help Matthew and me—not "just" to pray.

Within a week of my comment, they gave me an envelope. I could see that it was a card — another one among ninety or so, all assuring me that friends cared about me and were thinking of me. I placed the unopened envelope on the table beside my bed. I would enjoy Caroline's visit now and could look forward to opening it later, after she had gone.

"Aren't you going to open it?" Caroline's voice sounded almost hurt, but her eyes sparkled with excitement.

"Oh . . . all right then," I conceded. Wearily, I slit the long white envelope and pulled out the card.

Something slipped out from between the folds onto my blankets, followed by a ten-pound note. I handled the money and then picked up the other paper from between the folds. It was a check. I turned it over to read it: "Four hundred and ten pounds only."

I stared at the words incredulously. Caroline was almost dancing on the bed. She knew the wonderful freedom and pleasure of giving in response to God. She, and the whole group, had not held fund-raising events. They had prayed to God to help me; they had listened to Him; and they had responded by giving whatever they felt was right. They had managed to double a gift Matthew's mother had lovingly promised to us.

"You can have your holiday in the sun!" Caroline exclaimed, impatient with my stunned silence. Her voice was almost squeaking, such was her joy in giving.

I had just begun to believe what we had been given when Colin dropped by once again. About twice each day he showed his continuing care and support.

I handed him the envelope.

He was kneeling on the floor beside the bed, just as Tina had done in her turn. Now it was his turn to be silenced. His eyes moistened as he witnessed such love and involvement of Christian friends.

When others heard of the check, they, too, joined in with their prayerful contributions until we could have a really big vacation.

"If all you can do is lie down, then go and do that — but in the sun," they said.

So we did. After browsing through brochures, we took off. We had chosen a tiny island fifty miles from Madeira, with only one hotel and a long white beach. This was my longest spell out of the hospital. We felt free — free from hospital routines, visiting hours, telephone calls from caring relations. For almost two weeks we were together, alone.

Matthew's biggest problem now was stopping me from swimming! My natural love of water and sport, combined with the lure of the balmy turquoise water, almost overcame common sense. I lacked the physical strength to swim safely, so I had to be content with quick dips to cool off from the sun. And I developed a beautiful suntan.

But my honey-colored skin, which made me look so well, was misleading. The respite was not to last long.

4. Stay Here and Keep Watch With Me

Stay here and keep watch with me
(Matthew 26:38).

I accompanied Matthew to seminary in May. Our welcome back was wonderful. For some people it was like seeing me return from the dead—the last time they had seen me was at the communion service before the Easter holiday, when I had been pale and drawn.

"Jane—you look so much better! You look wonderful! You *are* so much better," they said. Perhaps neither they nor I realized how much my healthy-looking suntan belied my internal condition.

"You *still* look radiant, Jane. How are you?" That sort of comment came from those who took slightly more time to inquire how I felt, rather than presume that my appearance represented how I felt.

Those who knew I enjoyed a good joke grinned: "Trust you to wear a white blouse just to accentuate your tan." I twinkled in reply. Yes, I had to admit I did enjoy being the envy of so many people.

I was wearing a white blouse again a few days later when our hopes for a gradual convalescence suddenly plummeted.

It was during another Thursday evening communion service in the seminary chapel that the abdominal pain became much worse. When pain is severe, it is often hard to say that it is slightly better or slightly worse—pain is always bad! But this Thursday evening there was no doubt that it was intensifying. I resisted my first temptation to whisper to Matthew. If he were to suggest we leave, I didn't think I could get out of the chapel. Instead, I held on to a hope that it was a spasm which would pass.

I heard nothing of the service. My thoughts were entirely taken up with thoughts of how I could get out of the chapel without drawing attention to myself.

I glanced sideways toward the door. It was not too far away. But panic rose in me as I realized the row was filled with people between me and the door. They were all men, too. *They're sure to think I am a sissy for leaving,* I speculated. *So I can't go.*

Graham, Matthew's tutor who had remained so close to us throughout my illness, was on Matthew's right. *Graham will think I'm unable to bear the idea that I am no longer the center of attention. He'll think that I'm only trying to attract attention now if I walk out bent double.* I was paralyzed by fear of being thought a fraud. Graham had been so caring toward us—I did not want to lose his support by giving him the opportunity to suspect that I was simply exaggerating my symptoms.

This time, though, the physical pain overrode my fears of being branded a psychiatric wreck. Waiting for it to pass did not work. The pain got worse until it reached a level I had not previously known existed.

A hymn began. I prodded Matthew.

"Can't get up," I garbled. Once again, every word cost me extra breath, and every breath meant more pain searing through me.

"Well, just sit through the hymn, silly," Matthew replied vaguely without looking at me.

I am normally happy when Matthew can enjoy times of release from being weighed down by the solemnity of my suffering. I felt sorry in chapel that I had to shatter his freedom and make him realize what I meant.

I slipped my hand into his, ready to try to explain.

Matthew was shocked to feel the clamminess of my hand. It was wet with perspiration.

He took my hand and then looked at me, questioning. "Oh, my dear Jane!" he whispered, seeing my face for the first time. I wondered what my face looked like, for it certainly precipitated an immediate reaction from him!

The piano introduction was over and everyone else stood up to sing. I was thankful for the small element of privacy that brought, for now I could be seen only by one row of people between me and the door.

"Come on." Matthew left no room for discussion as to whether I should leave the service.

"Can't get up." I began to be distressed by my helplessness.

Matthew lifted me and continued to take much of my weight as he accompanied me toward the vestry door. Most of the men were immersed in their singing but as I passed Graham I was again tormented by the fear of him thinking I was a fraud. Despite the terrible pain, despite my need to concentrate on every move toward the door, I somehow mustered a big smile for him. It was a bluff, aimed at keeping him from any suspicion of what was going on.

The effect of that smile was twofold. First, it protected me in my embarrassment at being so vulnerable. I did not know how I would cope with being visibly outfaced by pain. But while I was successful in avoiding "making a fuss," I was also cutting Graham off from the opportunity to know the truth, to care or help. It was a high price for me to pay. What I wanted most was — and is — for people to show they care. They cannot cure the pain, but they can comfort me within it. And, like it or not, I needed help.

Once the chapel door was shut behind us, Matthew looked for a chair. There was none.

"What shall we do?" he asked.

"Must tell Richard." He was the only one who could really do anything to help. I knew something had happened inside me that Richard should know about. Even though it was evening, there was no doubt that he must see me immediately.

I leaned forward over the table with my arms outstretched and rested my head on my hands. This was the only thing I could do to find any relief at all; yet I knew I could not stay there. As I raised myself again, my eye was caught by the reflection of myself in the mirror ahead. With some horror I saw that my suntan had suddenly disappeared, replaced by ashen white.

I knew I had to move on and, leaning heavily on Matthew, I staggered to the staircase. I sat down on one of the steps.

"What do you want me to do?" Matthew repeated.

This time he realized I was beyond being able to think as calmly and sensibly as he.

"Can't move," was all I could say in a staccato voice. "I simply can't." I nearly panicked at finding myself so helpless, so paralyzed by pain. And yet, strange as it may seem, in the midst of all this trauma I was still aware of a deep peace and acceptance undergirding me and I just sat rigid on the step. "Shall I phone Richard or the G.P., or get an ambulance?" Matthew suggested.

I couldn't have an ambulance coming for me while I was conscious! Matthew's question caused me to muster all my strength again. Slowly, carefully, I pulled myself up and managed to descend a few stairs. Matthew did not press me for an answer, though he must have wondered what would happen next. He swallowed all his own questions in order to stay with my pace in the whole saga, patient at my side.

By the time we reached the bottom of the stairs I had agreed to one of his suggestions. We would seek help at the caring home of the president of the seminary and his wife, Di.

I could trust Di. She would not think of judging me as a fraud; she would simply care. As our short spurts of progress brought us toward her house, I had some "carrot" of hope for help. Di did not disappoint us. Her welcome gave us no indication that she and her daughters were in the middle of eating when we rang the bell. It was almost as if she were expecting us.

"Jane!" She held her arm out to me in a quiet, helping gesture. "You're coming in to lie down?" She looked to Matthew for confirmation.

Hands helped me to a comfortable chair. The kind smiles and caring eyes of everyone merged into a spinning haze of pain. I began to shiver and shake uncontrollably. Blankets were fetched and wrapped around me.

What a granny I must look like was the only thought which penetrated my daze. Then Di was sponging my face and neck with soothing warm water, and my hands were submerged and the water was gently swished over them. Allowing them to float eased away some of the shock.

The water itself was a therapy; the tender care with which it was done was even more so.

From behind my closed eyes I heard Matthew telephoning in the hall. He was having difficulty getting help. The G.P. was refusing to leave her clinic to come. Richard was on the golf course and, though his wife had offered to send a message to him, it would be some time before he could do anything.

Matthew returned. He and Di were discussing plans. Di left for the chapel to get a doctor. Immediate help was needed until Richard could be contacted.

Cathy, a doctor who was married to one of the other seminary students, though whisked out from the chapel service, was unflustered. She did not persist unnecessarily with her examination of me. She assessed what injection I needed, and drove off promptly to fetch some.

By the time Colin returned home, the morphine had begun to work. He had not seen the various exits from the chapel service earlier. He leapt up the steps two at a time into his house as usual and strode straight into the room.

He soon switched his quick mind. "You're not feeling so good, Jane?" He perched himself on a chair. He always had time to listen when there was a real need.

"Not wonderful," was my reply. "Silly, isn't it?" and I tried to chuckle lightly to deflect the heaviness I felt.

Someone else filled in details of the hunt for medical assistance, while my mind drifted in a morphine blur. Colin took it all in. He stayed with us the remainder of the evening, suspending whatever else he had planned to do. Both Matthew and I noticed appreciatively the sacrifice of his time—most especially because we knew how immensely busy he is. Yet he stopped for those precious hours, simply to be with us.

He was not even "helping" us formally by counseling us. At one stage, I remember Di's voice as she re-entered the room: "What are you all doing, chatting away about these irrelevant things, while Jane's here, feeling as she is?"

Visitors who had dropped in to see me on their way home from college (the rumor of my whereabouts had spread already) sank back into a rather shameful silence. The men had been enjoying an animated discussion together. But Colin was unabashed.

"Nonsense!" he said. "Jane doesn't want us to go on about her miseries, nor does she fancy holding the floor herself as a present. We're being most thoughtful, keeping the conversation going as she would want to happen and allowing her to do her own thing over there. Isn't that right, Jane?"

"I'll give you a $B+$ for a great speech," I grinned, wondering to myself how I had mustered the breath for such a long sentence. Perhaps it was worth it for a bit of banter. To continue to be game for fun, even while continuing in pain, was to keep being me.

And anyway, Colin's answer was right. All I could do was lie limply on the sofa and allow any conversation to drift over me. Soon the visitors left, the girls retired upstairs and only Colin and Di sat on with Matthew and me until the late May twilight.

Tension mounted as the minutes ticked by. We were still waiting for at least a message from Richard. If we did not hear soon, the effect of the injection would diminish and my state of shock might worsen seriously. Cathy had insisted she would return within two hours to attend me if I was still not in the hospital, but I loathed troubling her. I felt I was a thorough nuisance and wished I could pull myself together.

Our speculations were stalled by a visit from Graham, who had been seated to Matthew's right in the chapel service. He had only just heard where I was and why.

"Why on earth didn't you get Matthew to fetch me out of chapel?" he asked, half chuckling at my refusal to give in, half hurt (I suspect) that I seemed not to trust him. "We could have carried you down the stairs together."

I curled up at the notion. "Please don't be hurt," I pleaded. It was not he who was not trustworthy, but I who did not dare to trust anyone lest I be thought a fraud.

Like Colin, Graham suppressed any thoughts for himself. "Are you afraid, Jane?" As always, he could discern the most important issue.

I paused before answering. His questions were always worth thinking about. "I'm so completely taken up in coping with the present that I'm not looking ahead." The morphine was now taking effect. My words could be less staccato, my sentences less brief.

"But now that I'm asking you?" he pursued. My thoughts raced on to what would be decided about me during the coming night, inevitably in the hospital.

"I suppose I am . . . But I'm all right."

Graham knew about my experience of deep inner peace, which had risen out of my acceptance that even this pain might be under God's hand. He dared to dig deeper. "What do you fear most of all?"

I let my mind consider for a moment all the various possibilities that lay ahead of me. What did I fear the most among them? Certainly it was not the possibility of dying which made me fearful—that would have brought so much relief from the pain that it was a welcome idea. And that, I realized, was the clue to my worst fear.

"Continuation of pain with no prospect of relief," I said numbly. "As you know, I fear another anesthetic, especially with the memory of not being fully asleep last year before they started doing things to me."

I shuddered as I remembered the tubes being put down my throat, my body being handled as if I were not conscious, and the horror of being unable to move or show any sign that I was still awake.

"And I fear the weakness and the long, long uphill struggle of recovering from a big operation. But those would be just about bearable if they were successful and worthwhile." I paused to think about the meaningful type of pain, such as labor pain, which, though intense and dreadful at the time, is normally forgotten as soon as it brings forth its purpose — a healthy baby. But this was in stark contrast to my suffering.

"It's the thought of pain with no end, no purpose, no fruit, which is so difficult." Even as I said it I knew that Graham had helped me by pushing me so far. To be afraid to examine my inner fears was to allow them to plant roots. To bring them out into the open was to bring them into the light of God.

Graham understood.

"God doesn't make any mistakes, Jane." How often he had reinforced that truth to me.

"No. I don't feel this is His mistake." Talking was giving me more confidence in God's will.

Graham smiled. "How are you so sure of that?"

"Because God is in it." I myself was amazed to find within my mind and soul a deep-down tranquility, even in the face of immense pain. "It's accompanied by such peace, such an assurance of Him with me, that I know it's not His mistake." Whatever was to follow that night, I determined to accept God's will — I knew I was in His hands. "I just wish I could get comfortable now."

And Graham, in his wisdom, could accept what I was expressing. There is a tension between acceptance of God's will even when He does not promise to give us a comfortable life, and the hard grind of enduring suffering when it comes.

I was alone again with Colin and Di, and there was a quietness in the room, although the warm hominess was somewhat marred. The increasing urgency with which we awaited the telephone's ring pressed in upon us. Outside, darkness was falling quickly and the air chilled. Di tucked my blankets around me again and lit the small lamps on the shelf. As she bent down, soft shadows were cast across her cheeks. It was then I noticed the anxiety in her face.

Suddenly everyone was jerked away from apprehensive speculation. For an uncertain moment, Matthew looked quickly to his host, then he leaped across to answer the shrill telephone himself.

However long the hours of waiting had been, however many times I had rehearsed Richard's reaction in my mind, I was still surprised to hear the stark reality of the words: "We're to meet Richard at the hospital in fifteen minutes." Matthew was leaning round the door, relaying instructions. "Will you manage to go in our car, or should he send an ambulance?"

"Oh, car please." At least Matthew would be careful to drive gently and avoid potholes in the road. "Do I really have to go, though?"

Matthew smiled, withdrew to the phone and let the door close behind him. Colin rose to find my coat; Di came toward me to help me get up from the sofa. I gathered that I had asked a silly question which warranted no reply.

Somehow I managed to stand up, but however much I tried I could not straightened myself completely. I felt humiliated to be so stooped and bent in front of friends whom I respected. I imagined that if only I could make enough effort, I would succeed in looking normal.

Inch by inch I struggled across the room, wondering at each step how I could cross the few feet to the door. Colin's face was very compassionate as he opened the door for me. Then, seeing outside to the slight ramp I had to negotiate to get into the car, I almost felt too daunted. I swallowed hard and gripped the low garden wall.

Matthew was beside me, encouraging me but still allowing me to feel independent. Colin must have felt impotent, unable to help me further. "Would it not be best if we lifted you?"

I shook my head. "I'm okay," was the most I could say. To give in would have been to fail in what I thought I was expected to "achieve." Thus I willed myself determinedly to get to the car: *Shuffle one foot forward. You must do it. Take a breath. Now the other foot. Don't crack now.*

Matthew closed the car door and started the engine. Colin and Di were silhouetted in their doorway against the glowing lights of their warm home. As the car turned, the headlights swished round to illuminate their faces. They smiled and waved. Their hearts were with us.

I clenched my hands as the car moved forward at last. Still the two figures remained on the threshold, gazing out at us. They waited and watched until we were out of sight. Even when we could no longer see them we knew that they were with us in spirit, as we drove into the darkness.

While I suffered, they suffered with me.

5. If One Suffers, All Suffer

If one part suffers, every part suffers with it;
if one part is honored, every part rejoices with it
(1 Corinthians 12:26).

As I was being driven away from Colin's house, something important was happening to me. Weak though I was, my body aching and groaning, I was nevertheless growing as a person. I was aware, more than previously, of the "fellowship of suffering." Out of love for me, Matthew and many friends were suffering with me—entering into my pain. And I, in turn, was aware of them—more tuned in to their vulnerability and need, more able to understand them and to be a more genuine, sympathetic friend.

It was hard for Matthew to turn from my bedside and leave the hospital. Not that he had much energy left, for it was already past midnight. But he did not like to walk away when I was in such anguish. He felt that not staying was almost like turning his back on me. Was he betraying me? It had all gone on for so long, it had gradually become an unconscious part of our life. I was living in pain, he was living with it. Or maybe he was living in pain himself, his different from mine.

When Matthew was gone, my mind was full of the haunting scenes of that evening. Uppermost was the vision of Richard's face, solemn, unmoving. What had he been thinking? What more might he do to help me? Was there any further treatment to which he could resort?

Richard had shown no signs of emotion. He had proceeded in a calm, business-like manner. Perhaps he, too, felt a measure of distress but dared not show it lest it cloud his clinical judgment. I was the patient, he the helper. He would surely be failing if he became a victim of my suffering as well.

"I'm very sorry," he had said numbly. "Just to complicate matters, I'm afraid I'm off to France for the weekend tomorrow." His eyes fixed thoughtfully on the shiny hospital floor.

A weekend? That seemed an unbearably long time. Richard must have guessed from the fear in my eyes that I could not imagine how I would keep going for so long. I wanted to be able to give up, yet I did not know how. Whatever I did, however much I sank down into the bed, I was dominated by pain.

"I must get the professor's opinion," he had announced, walking purposefully to the telephone.

Suddenly, things began to move. After weeks and months of not knowing what to do, the medical profession seemed galvanized into action. The professor and another surgeon were brought in to give their opinions. They hesitated to operate. They could not be certain what exactly they hoped to achieve. Once again I was pumped full of injections – a constant infusion of antibiotics and even vitamins. Once again I was lying pale, listless and exhausted by pain.

Then one day they had a case conference, right by my bed. The dynamics were strained. Richard, back from his holiday weekend, was technically in overall charge of me, but he was nevertheless junior to the professor. It was difficult for him to express his surprise that another laparotomy had not been done. His judgment was based more on how ill he sensed I was than on specific medical tests. He was very concerned. In comparison, the professor seemed intent on appearing relaxed about my condition. He had reinforced that most firmly by strolling into the ward forty minutes late.

By this time, Richard was seething. Perhaps, again, he was subconsciously suffering. He had to endure the impotence and possibly the self-doubt that were part of an inability to make me better. He barely raised his eyes to greet the latecomer. It had not crossed any of our minds that even the professor could have felt pain from the whole situation — that his difficult attitude might have been a tell-tale sign of his own uneasiness.

"You've resorted to surgical intervention unnecessarily in the past," came the stinging accusation.

There was a pause. Richard refused to rise to such a bait. The professor flicked through my case notes. "Look at this histology report. You removed 'normal tissue' last time." He thrust the brown folder into Richard's hands.

Tension rose as Richard's very competence was called into question. "I am telling you . . . " Richard paused a moment to steady his voice, "I saw what I removed and I can still see it now. What I removed was abnormal, an obvious cause of severe abdominal pain. Jane was much improved for eight months after surgery, until this acute peritonitis flared up again in February."

Only the sound of their heavy footsteps punctuated the silence between them as they approached my bed. Each man's face appeared firm and hard. Matthew's hand closed more tightly around my thin wrist. He was tense too, waiting to hear of their decision.

Richard had almost been silenced by the conference; he simply nodded kindly to Matthew. It was the professor who, accustomed to acting as chairman, gave their report. Involuntarily I drew breath as I listened.

"As you know, Jane has had a lot of problems with peritoneal inflammation." He was addressing Matthew rather than me. "She seems to be having continued pain despite our conservative medical treatment on drugs."

"Conservative?" questioned Richard in a whisper, which was nevertheless an interruption. His eyes turned to my intravenous infusion with its two lots of strong-dose antibiotics. The appropriateness of his query succeeded in causing irritation in the midst of a rather pompous speech.

"And therefore," the voice continued more loudly, "we have decided that there is no course of action left to us except further surgery."

Matthew was uncomfortable at being so passive, especially in this atmosphere. The only active thing he could do was speak, even though it was a question.

"What do you propose doing?"

My heart beat faster, harder.

The professor hesitated slightly before meeting Matthew's uncertain gaze. "Clear the pelvis." He cleared his throat, turned away and walked a few steps to the end of my bed. Was he withdrawing from some sort of suffering Matthew's anguish caused in him? Then, straightening up, he faced Matthew again. Retreating to the safety of his familiar role, he launched into a verbose explanation, as if he were lecturing students. Apparently when pain threatened to disturb his equanimity, he distanced himself by using academic language.

"A total pelvic clearance . . . " he began. I could not listen. With my knowledge as a midwife I needed no explanation anyway. He had said only what I had expected. He meant a hysterectomy, but he could not bring himself to use the word. "Total pelvic clearance" sounded much more remote.

A host of different emotions welled up inside me, each one clamoring for my attention. I lay back on the pillows numbly, allowing the whole conversation to go over my head.

They could have been discussing anyone, anything. Where was their care and concern? Had it been completely swallowed up in the unspoken rivalry between the two specialists? I could have been Exhibit A, providing a useful example of what the professor was explaining. And Matthew could have been a young schoolboy as they bombarded him with statements. "You'll have to understand that if we go ahead, this means no children. Removing a uterus means removing all childbearing potential."

I felt like a cow, a machine, anything but a person. I wanted to shout out, "Shut up! I have feelings; haven't you?" But maybe it was precisely because he found it so hard that the professor adopted his unfortunate manner. Maybe it felt safer for him to sound objective, clinical, detached. Maybe to have shown more care would have made him more aware of the suffering my pain caused within him.

The following month or so has now become a blur. I have probably blotted things from my mind in my subconscious drive not to dwell on such painful memories. In a sense, this was the end for me, the end of so much . . . so many hopes, so many dreams, so many expectations. Yet it was the beginning of the end of more important things, too. The profound illness which had engulfed me for the four months since February would always leave its scar, but its terrifying intensity was soon to recede.

Only a few things haunt me, standing out as they do among what, otherwise, my mind refuses to recall. First there was the terrible waiting, waiting for the appointed day of the operation. In the climate of relationships with the professor, Richard had made a resolve. He would not carry out this operation without the professor there. He knew how much the professor's opinion was disadvantaged until he had seen with his own eyes the state of my insides. Only by this means would he be led to respect Richard's judgment once again.

Despite my frail state, both physically and no doubt emotionally as I faced the operation, I was not to avoid being caught in the midst of the friction. Richard and the professor were not seeing eye to eye, and my operation seemed a timely opportunity for them to engage in a duel.

At last the activity around me increased as the preparations for my operation began. I knew so well the humiliating procedures which, though mundane, heralded surgery.

"You mustn't drink anything now, Mrs. Grayshon." The nurses were busily sticking tubes everywhere— yes, everywhere.

"I'm just going to give you a little enema, Mrs. Grayshon." *Little?* I thought.

"I'm just going to put a little tube into your bladder, Mrs. Grayshon." Why did they keep using the word *little?* To try to make the overall problem seem smaller?

"I'm just going to give you a little shave, Mrs. Grayshon."

Everything they did was all too familiar to me. I'd traveled this way so often before, I could have spoken their words of "reassurance" myself.

When at last the waiting was over, I lay in the anesthetic room before being put to sleep. Wherever I looked, my eyes seemed to fall upon something which held nightmarish memories for me. The trolley with a ventilator reminded me of when I could not breathe for myself; the clear bottles of drugs seemed to reinforce that this was my seventh operation; the needles seemed poised and ready to inflict once again that feeling of vulnerability which I dread with every anesthetic.

My eyes closed to try to escape the memories. Apprehensively I speculated once again on the outcome of this surgery. The form on which I had signed my consent had read: "Exploratory laparotomy [meaning a jolly good look inside my abdomen] possibly proceeding to total pelvic clearance." *Will things be bad enough for that?* I wondered. Or was I slightly better now? Might they find that the infection had resolved itself and I had little reason left for complaining of pain?

Richard had already gone through to the operating room. When I had seen him, he was twisting his fingers together nervously. He too was apprehensive. It was his professional expertise which was about to be exposed on the operating table. Would he be vindicated in his boss's eyes? I rubbed the cold sweat from my hands on the skimpy sheet draped over me. I wished this waiting would end.

At that moment the professor breezed in. I hardly recognized him at first. He was disguised in his surgery garb and I was peering through the haze of my pre-med injection. Then he spoke in his distinctive accent.

"Ah, well," he chuckled. "The truth will come out now, eh?"

"Pardon?" I was struggling to distinguish his words from behind his flimsy green facemask.

"I said, the truth will come out now," he repeated. I think he also muttered something about me looking bright-eyed and bushy-tailed. Was he saying I was a fraud?

No sooner had that question raced into my mind than the operating room's swinging door banged closed. He had gone. The anesthetist had taken my arm now and was already injecting his drug. The black rubber door squeaked open again. Richard popped his head around, only his dark eyes showing between mask and hat. They crinkled with a reassuring smile.

"See you in there," I heard him say. The buzzing in my ears dragged me into an oppressive sleep.

6. The Fellowship of Suffering

Carry each other's burdens
(Galatians 6:2)

From a great distance someone was calling me.

"Jane?"

My body was too heavy.

"Jane?"

My breathing felt labored.

"Jane?"

Oh, I was so weary.

"Can you hear me, Jane?"

Yes, I could hear. But I didn't want to hear. I was too tired. She couldn't have realized how badly I needed to sleep. Who was she, anyway?

I was standing in a field. I could smell flowers growing among the corn. They were stale. Every breath I took brought with it the stale smell. It was nauseating. Why was it not sweet? I breathed again.

I tried to turn away from the field of flowers. Whichever way I turned, it stretched ahead of me. I could not get away from it. And the smell once again swept over me. I had to draw another breath. It seemed I was filled with the foul smell. I was very sick.

Something cold and metallic was pushed under my chin. What was this? Perhaps I was not alone. Why could I not see anyone else?

The air was putrid now. If only I could escape the smell. I did not understand, then, that it was my own breath, heavy with the anesthetic gases, which I wanted to avoid.

"Jane? Can you take a big breath for me?" I wondered why I should want to take a big breath. That would increase the oppressive smell. It was enough to take my little gasps.

The voice altered. "Better give more oxygen," it whispered. A mask was pushed over my face. Its plastic aroma mingled with the stale flowers in my field. It made me even more trapped by the smell.

"You've had your operation, dear." My operation? Oh. Oh, I see. Yes, that's right. My operation. Well what had they found then? What had they done?

My questions faded as I drifted back to the field. The next minute (or so it seemed) I was being bumped and battered. I must be on a trolley, being wheeled along, I reasoned. Dit-dit. Elevator doors were crashed open. Dit-dit. Two more wheels crashed over the threshold into the elevator. Whirrrrr. The doors were opened again. Dit-dit. Dit-dit.

"You're back in the ward now, Jane." It was the friendly nurse speaking.

I nodded silently, my eyes still closed. Gradually my field faded, giving way to the slow assimilation of what was happening. I tried to ask questions. "What . . . ?" But my mouth would not work properly.

The nurse bent over me. She lacked no imagination as to how I felt. Her shoes made no clack when she walked. She was the sensitive kind of nurse.

"It's all over, Jane." Oh, if only that were true, I thought. And what had they actually found? What had they done?

"What . . . ?" was the only word I could muster.

The nurse understood. She was a gem. "They did what they feared they would have to do." Her discretion never faltered. She knew they were the ones to tell me; but she also honored the fact that I was ready to hear now. I had had a hysterectomy.

I nodded again, and drifted back to my field.

It was the professor's presence which I remember next. He had entered rather more stealthily than his confident approach in the anesthetic room before surgery.

He commented on the operation, repeating to me their findings. Everything has blurred into a smudge of memory now. I only remember one of his remarks. He asked innocently, "I expect you were in pain beforehand, were you, Jane?"

In pain? What could I say? Pain seemed such an underestimation of what I had experienced, such a glib word for such depth of agony. After all, I had felt that I would die.

"Yes, I was a little," I replied distantly. Words alone could never have formed an adequate answer for him, so I did not try.

I was a little more alert a few days later when Richard came again to discuss things with me. He did not hide his astonishment at my progress as I stood up and twirled around proudly. "The discomfort from this is nothing, compared . . . " I remarked with glee.

"You just be careful," he warned, but I could see from the gleam in his eye that he was both thrilled and relieved at my progress.

I had my questions for him, too. "Which one of you decided?" I asked, intrigued to learn how the dynamics had resolved between the two surgeons.

"Neither of us," came the cool measured reply. "As soon as we opened you up, the decision lay staring up at us on the table. There was no question in either of our minds."

Then Richard's face suddenly twinkled. "I got the pathology report back today," he told me. It said, "Normal tissue."

"Oh?" I was slightly confused. How could it be "normal" when Richard had only just told me how bad it looked? I looked up at him questioningly. Suddenly I saw the mischief in his face, and I understood. It *was* confusing; I *was* confusing medically. But that did not mean my illness could be denied, as some found it easy to suggest.

"I've left it on the professor's desk for him to find!" he ended. We both smiled, sharing the irony in silence.

But nobody had used the word "hysterectomy." While the phrase "total pelvic clearance" was accurate, it gave no indication of any loss I may have felt. So I tried not to feel any. I tried to be brave. I joined in the discussion about it as if I were strong and courageous like those men. Once again, my childhood years with my brothers served me very well. I had had much practice in suppressing any girlish, sissyish wallowing.

Until one evening when a familiar nurse was in charge of the ward. She was new to this ward, though I had once worked with her elsewhere. She must have found it difficult on this evening because our usual roles were reversed. I, more senior to her as a nurse, was now in bed; she was in a position to tell me what to do.

She bounded gaily into the room, obviously very pleased with herself. Her harsh voice grated on my ears. Her words pierced through at me, "I heard you had your hyst, dear," she said, smiling broadly.

It was as if the ground had been whisked from under my feet. I did not know what to say, or where to look. It would have hurt me too much to think. Instead, I still recall how enormous was my urge to do something to humiliate her back. She had marched in and trampled all over my feelings. I could only fantasize about picking up the jug of cold water from my locker and pouring it right over her head.

Everything about that nurse spoke of her care for herself more than for any patient. Her loud, smart shoes demonstrated that she preferred to look good than respect a sick person's need for quietness. Her stark makeup reflected the trouble she took to present an artificial image rather than genuine self-giving care.

She was relishing her opportunity to be a cut above me now that I was vulnerable. She had formerly hated my telling her off for smoking in the women's restroom. She never understood why I asked her to talk more gently to the patients. "A bit of light-hearted fun never did anyone any harm," she would retort.

The last thing I wanted that evening was a bit of light-hearted fun. For the first time I was being courageous enough to feel somewhat low. I suppose I was allowing the first waves of realization of what a hysterectomy meant to penetrate my heart. Now my loss was being devalued again, even by the "affectionate" abbreviation to "hyst."

I think I have never fully accepted how crushed I was. I have never really gotten over other people's avoidance of the word "hysterectomy." I know that, since then, I have rarely used the word myself. It hurts less if I refer to "the operation in 1980."

I lacked compassion at the time, but now I realize that the nurse only sounded harsh because she too was in pain. She did not know what to say or how to cope with my suffering. She tried to hide under light-hearted words, but her awkward pain was still there. Unfortunately, I just happened to be the one to bear the inappropriateness of her brashness.

Over and over again, my pain caused others to suffer with me: Matthew, the doctors, the nurses, our family and our friends who cared for me and who wanted me to be healed. It hurt them all to see me suffer. The pain of others often acted as a hindrance which concealed the care they wanted to express. I, in turn, found that hurtful when I felt so much in need of their care. But shortly afterwards, a letter from my friend Geoff seemed to explain it all, and helped me to understand much better:

> Your suffering is painful to many, Jane, and they cannot cope because they love you so much. So, because of the pain, they cannot express the depth of love they are longing to share with you and which you are longing to receive. Accept the love of many, for it exists, and be motivated to live for the sake of all those who cry out but make no sound.

No one suffers in isolation. Within the fellowship of suffering there is an opportunity to grow in our ability to read one another aright in order to reach out to one another appropriately. I had thought that those who make no sound had forsaken me, but Geoff taught me to look beyond what people say — or fail to say.

My pilgrimage through suffering was surely not fruitless. It was teaching me how to reach out and truly identify with the reality of other people's situations. I felt humbled to think that through all this I might become a more useful channel for God's love.

As the days progressed I began to recover slowly from the operation. I could see the relief on the faces of those who suffered through this long trial with me. Everyone was rejoicing. I had avoided death, but was it all gain that I had been given life? Still I was weak, and very much aware of it. Wouldn't it have been better if things had turned out differently? Was it not true that "to die is gain"?

PART TWO

Living
in Pain

7. To Live Is Christ, and To Die Is Gain

For to me, to live is Christ
and to die is gain
(Philippians 1:21).

I wanted to be a more useful channel for God's love. And yet so much of the time life appeared to be such a burden.

The long, uphill struggle toward recovery after an operation is still vivid to me at this moment. As I write, I am again recovering from yet more surgery. Another . . . and another. The word *surgery* is so simply written, but each time it denotes a particular experience of seemingly unending suffering. In one sense it's as if I have a nightmare which has repeated itself yet again. Only I do not dream it—I have to live it. And therein lies my agony. If it were a nightmare, I would hope to wake up and discover the freedom of the pain's absence. How often that has been my greatest longing. And how often it has seemed that to die would indeed be gain for me.

I know that I am not alone. Others — many others — in this life long only for release. They feel utterly trenched in, and surrounded by their own form of pain — physical or other.

Last month a woman I knew suddenly collapsed. Within two weeks she died. At the funeral I watched her husband and three teenage children. Their faces, though mourning, were serenely radiant. They were confident that Sylvia was now with her Lord in a place where she knew no more pain, no more tears.

I mustn't long for that, I repeated over and over to myself. I clenched my fists tightly inside my coat pocket.

I looked at the wooden coffin. It was insignificant; nothing. It reminded me of a book I had read in which the Little Prince had described a dead body. "Like an old abandoned shell," he had said. "There is nothing sad about old shells."

No, there was nothing sad about Sylvia's dead body. Those who were left were sad in their loss, of course, but not Sylvia. She had only gained. It was not the coffin which was difficult for me to look at. It was myself.

I was still encased in my body, my pain. I was like that Little Prince before his death. He had said, "I cannot carry this body with me. It is too heavy." That's how I felt, too.

That day at the funeral, I felt particularly burdened by the heaviness of my body. It was less than a week since I had seen a new consultant in London. I did not realize it then, but I was heading for another bout of peritonitis. I had hoped that as a result of this consultation a new treatment might be suggested to alleviate the worsening symptoms. I had thought a clever new "bigwig" might be able to cure me.

The consultation had hardly begun before my hope was torn from me. "You're a problem," were the doctor's first words to me. "What do you expect but pain, with a history like yours?"

Sylvia's funeral service followed too soon after that. I was not in a position to cope with the stark comparison between the abandoned shell in that coffin and my living body, pulsating with pain.

I wrestled with myself throughout the service. While others wept silently in sorrow, I fought back my tears. I had to keep control. I knew that if I shed one tear, it would not just be a quiet little sniffle. I would have sobbed uncontrollably. I would have prostrated myself before my Lord, my Father. I would have wept on and on, unable to bear this spotlight on years of exasperation.

"I can't bear this, Lord. I can't. I *can't!*" I would have cried. "What are You asking of me? What are You doing to me? It's too much. If pain is my life, I don't want it. I don't want life."

And it was not just because of my own pain that I felt distraught. "Lord, look at Matthew quietly bearing so much. When I look at his eyes, I see reflected in them the whole story of my suffering. I feel so helpless. I am the main character acting out this saga, yet I have no means of altering the plot. Lord, stop it, please!"

But I didn't let go like that. Somehow I managed to maintain some composure, some unselfish serenity. But it was hard. At that moment everything seemed hard — all my pain, life itself, even God.

And there, all the time, stood that coffin. Dead. Nothing was hard any more for that old abandoned shell. To die was gain.

It felt frustrating that this, so nearly, had been me. Not once, but at least three times I have nearly died.

The thought brought no fear, but as we rose to sing a hymn the vivid memories of those times flooded back with a certain horror . . .

The occasion uppermost in my mind was in 1979. I was on the operating table in surgery when I suddenly realized I was able to hear all that was going on around me. Somehow I was amazingly detached, as if I were an interested observer of everything. I listened to the tense voices which surrounded me:

"She needs more oxygen."

"Her pulse rate is very high."

"Her blood pressure's dropped even further."

Then a man's authoritative boom: "Get some plasma. Quickly, nurse." The sound of wooden clogs on the stone floor receded, running, then returned.

"Where *is* the plasma?" she asked, flustered.

Poor soul, I had mused, remembering my own early days as a student nurse learning the whereabouts of equipment on each ward. The man's voice was raised. "I don't care where the hell it is. Just get it. Quickly."

I felt detached from it all. I speculated why they wanted the plasma so quickly for me. I also knew where the plasma was. *On the second shelf, above the Dextrose solution,* I thought. But it didn't matter. I was all right. All this was going on, but somehow it didn't seem to affect me. I felt unburdened. Why were they worrying? I felt amazingly free and light.

"She's not breathing." It was the man's voice. What did it matter? I felt fine.

"Blood pressure's very low. Speed up that drip." Really, they were fussing. They didn't seem to know I could hear. Certainly they couldn't have known how well I felt.

"Jane? Jane?" There were those voices again. "Can you take a big breath, Jane?" No, I couldn't. Why bother? I was flying, floating, free.

"Pass my laryngoscope." The man's voice kept interrupting my freedom. Suddenly my chin was jerked upwards. Fingers pressed my jaw and throat. An enormous metal instrument was being pushed into my mouth, past my tonsils. I couldn't get away from it. I couldn't shout out for help.

The fiddling stopped, but their invasion into me had hardly begun. I felt myself involuntarily drawing a breath. Or was it breath? A heaviness fell upon me, infusing my whole being. Then, as suddenly as they had filled, my lungs emptied.

"Good," came the voice. Good? The man was so wrong. This was not "good." I felt much worse now. I resented the heaviness, the burden of breathing. He had just caused me to lose the freedom and lightness which I had experienced for the first time ever. I felt claustrophobic, trapped, pressed in by the tubes now being tied into my mouth with a bandage around my head.

Then I heard the click-hum of another machine. As its hum crescendoed, I felt my lungs fill again. Click-hum. They emptied. A new dread came over me. I had been put on a ventilator . . .

In church, the hymn was almost over now. My eyes turned again toward Sylvia's family. They too knew the distinctive click-hum of a ventilator. Sylvia's breathing had needed assistance for a number of days before she died.

I wanted to reassure them. *There's no terror in dying*, I would have said. *You just feel ill. It's like feeling ill with the flu, except that you don't get better just temporarily. Once you die you become completely whole and well, face to face with Jesus. Permanently.*

The aspect of being face to face with Jesus was very important to me. Each time I have nearly died, I have been conscious of Jesus very close to me—so close that I would hardly have been surprised if His presence had become a physical thing. He would have reached out and taken my hand. For onlookers I suppose that would have been the moment of my death, but for me it would have been the beginning of true life.

I recalled another occasion in 1980 when I had been full of eager anticipation of Jesus actually coming to take me by the hand. I had told some friends about this time the day before Sylvia died.

"I was full of expectancy and hope. Matthew and I had been given a distinct vision of the place to which we were sure I was going." I tingled with excitement as I talked, reminding myself of what still awaited me.

"It was a picture of me as Jesus' bride. Angels were forming a corridor as they stood waiting to see the Bridegroom come and lead His bride through that corridor. All the angels were craning their necks to see the beauty of the bride. Jesus was proud to take His bride before His Father."

"Where did you get this picture from?" asked my friends, greatly moved by the imagery.

"A visiting preacher at Matthew's seminary," I replied. I thought back to the visit of this man. "At the time of his visit we had no idea what lay ahead during the school year, but we did know his words had a special ring of truth."

My friends marveled as they listened. For them this was a fresh, exciting way to think about dying. They were immensely reassured as they thought of Sylvia so close to death.

But for me? The prophetic words, speaking of the release of death into fullness and wholeness of life, seemed to heighten the distress of living on.

Yet it was no use comparing my pain with others. Sylvia's suffering had been so worthwhile. It was leading her to her death, where she would see God face to face. She could be thankful even for the actual pain, because it was acting as a vehicle to carry her to the place where God will wipe away every tear.

Thinking of Sylvia made me long for the comfort of the nearness of dying, of God's nearness, of the promise of a wonderful, permanent future. It was easy for me to be convinced by the truth that "to die is gain." I could clearly understand that I would discover eternal gain in death. It was much more difficult, however, to welcome the other half of that verse:"For to me to live is Christ." It was a struggle for me to understand how to find Christ in my life, even life with so much pain and suffering.

I found in myself a reaction near to bitterness. I had been so near to this wonderful reception in which Sylvia was rejoicing—and yet so far. Would it not have been an appropriate ending to a long saga of unexplained suffering if I had died triumphantly? But this was not part of God's plan for my life. Jesus did not come to take me by the hand and lead me with joy to His Father. He did not give the release we had anticipated. Instead, He called me to stay in my shell. He has called me to remain, living in pain.

Perhaps He has led me gently, but I cannot say it always feels gentle. The full force of realizing that He wants me to face this second-best place—on earth—can still be devastating. At such times I desperately need to be reassured by the Lord that His way and His timing are perfect.

Once I received exactly such reassurance. Lying in the hospital one day in 1980, semi-conscious, semi-drugged, I suddenly became aware of a great clarity of mind. I knew without a doubt that the thoughts in my head were very important. Reaching for a pen and a scrap of old tissue paper, I began to write, phrase by phrase. I did not know the next sentence until I had written the first.

It was as though God were directly giving me His words of comfort for the darkness which was to follow:

> You long for death because that is where you know I'll be. In fact the end is not death, but when you reach the end of your resources — where you cannot cope, you cannot bear any more. That is where I am . . .

> Therefore prepare yourself for this end, first of all by recognizing that it exists — that you will feel desperate and lonely. Then, while you are cool and rational, see ahead that I will be there . . .

> You cannot long for this end because it is too dreadful, too dark. But it's reassuring to know that this is where you meet more fully with Me . . . So, Jane, I do not expect you to look forward to these times, or to look back on them with joy. But you needn't dread them so much. I understand. Remember My hour in Gethsemane?

Arriving at home after Sylvia's funeral, I went straight upstairs. I thumbed through my drawer of precious pieces of paper until I found these words. Hungrily, I read them over and over again. Yes, today was one of those times about which God had spoken. I felt at the end of my resources, unable to cope. Assuredly, to die would be gain. But Christ was not only to be found in death. I relaxed a little as I accepted the assurance that God was nonetheless with me, however hard that *felt* for me to believe. The gospel does not simply say that God can rescue me out of my suffering — He can rescue me *in* it. If it was God's will for me to die, then Christ was to be found there as well.

Kneeling with my Bible, I turned to the beatitudes. "How blest are those who know their need of God," I read. That was me all right; I knew my need of God. "The kingdom of Heaven is theirs."

Then there was my favorite Psalm: "As a hart longs for flowing streams, so longs my soul for thee, O God" (Psalm 42:1). These verses certainly summarized my longing. But I needed more. I needed to hear some words of love or reassurance from God. I turned to the book of Isaiah and started reading in chapter 43. I lifted up my head and closed my eyes. I tried to accept and absorb the love of God as I pondered His Word, particularly the fourth verse.

I knew that belief in this verse was the only way I could endure living here on earth in pain. If I could really accept this verse as God speaking to me here and now, I would be able to know without doubt not only that "to die is gain," but also, "to live is Christ."

In silence I remained kneeling, alone before God, allowing His Word to speak to me personally: "You are precious in my eyes, and honored, and I love you" (Isaiah 43:4).

8. You Are Precious

*Since you are precious and honored in my sight,
and because I love you, I will give men
in exchange for you, and people
in exchange for your life
(Isaiah 43:4).*

It was August 1980 and I was much stronger after my operation. I was eagerly looking forward to another retreat to a convent where Matthew and I had spent three helpful weekends the previous year. The "total pelvic clearance" six weeks previously had served to stop the downward spiral of my illness and, to everyone else's relief, I was gradually regaining health and strength. However, there was still something lacking. Life was not wonderful. I had none of my old enthusiasm to enter into life fully, and I didn't understand why.

When we arrived at the retreat in Hertfordshire, I felt happy enough. We were warmly welcomed by the five Carmelite sisters whom we had come to know during our earlier visits. They were the Sisters of the Love of God, who saw their calling as spreading God's love throughout the world in prayer. They each sought to let God's love be made bigger in themselves. That love certainly spread to us in the welcome we received. As they showed Matthew and me to our separate little rooms I was full of anticipation that our three days there would help me feel restored in every way.

Sister Rachel and I discussed a few details about the silent meals and other practical matters, then she left to "allow me to enjoy the peace and stillness."

Suddenly I felt terribly alone. I had expected to find quietness, rest and peace in the silence. Instead, I found confusion. My mind was full of thoughts and feelings all clamoring loudly for my attention.

What was wrong with me? I had been seriously ill, on the brink of dying, but I had come through. I had made good progress and was well on the way to recovery. Surely I ought to be rejoicing with all those who had prayed for this healing. Why was my heart not full of praise and thankfulness to God? I decided to take a stroll in the extensive grounds. Perhaps being outside would take me out of myself, away from the drab simplicity of my room.

I sat down on a wooden bench beside the fish pond. The water glistened in the summer sun. To the right and behind, the kitchen garden stretched down the slope, all methodically laid out with vegetables. Beyond, huge brown nets enclosed further neat rows of fruit bushes. Everything I saw was ordered and calm. Closing my eyes to enjoy the sun's balmy rays, I tried to absorb the peacefulness. I heard the sound of the birdsong, interrupted only by the gentle scratching noise of a sister's hoe working at the well-tilled earth.

I thought back to one of my previous visits to the convent. I had been thoroughly satisfied with life then—on the crest of a wave with my achievements. I had just been appointed to a very good position as a nursing sister doing research, working alongside the university professor and two consultants. This early promotion put me in a good position for career advancement.

I had also won a national award from the Royal College of Nursing for an essay, and had been made to feel very important as a special guest at a reception in the lavish rooms of the Royal College in London. The occasion had led to the offer of a contract to write a nursing textbook. At the age of twenty-four I felt thrilled and honored. I seemed to have a valuable contribution to make in life. Through my achievements I felt that my life was worthwhile and that therefore I was precious.

I reflected on how much my thinking had changed during that particular weekend at the retreat. Having arrived so full of self-esteem, I was brought down to earth with a jolt on the first morning, A note had been pushed under my door. I recognized the handwriting to be Mo's. She was another student who had come with us from Matthew's college. She had copied one simple poem for me to meditate upon during the course of our silence:

> I wait for you, my child.
> I desire your love
> More than anything else you can give Me.
> Not your service
> Not your struggling and trying to please Me
> Or to please others.
> I want you to love Me;
> To love Me with all your heart, mind, soul,
>   strength.
> This is the first commandment,
> And matters more than all else besides.
> I need your love, fellowship, devotion and worship.
> I want you to be single-minded in this one thing.
> My Spirit is within you
> To enable you,
> To empower you,
> To fill your heart with love.
>
> I desire this not sometimes
> But always.

The poem had stopped me in my tracks. It suggested to me that God would be more pleased to see my relationship with Him deepen, than to see me doing wonderful things with my God-given talents. "I desire your love more than anything else you can give Me" — more, even, than my achievements for Him. Who I am was more important to Him than what I do or achieve in life.

As I recalled that previous stay, something seemed to fall into place in my mind. *Could it be,* I wondered as I got up to walk again through the grounds, *that I had allowed myself to forget the lessons I learned through Mo's poem? Had I been lulled back into the way our society thinks of people's worth, and away from God's perspective?* That would certainly explain why I felt unhappy in my own company.

In strong contrast to the high sense of self-esteem I enjoyed then, I did not now have any "achievements" to be pleased about. I had spent the past six months passively enduring illness. During that time I had had no chance to "earn" any feeling of being special in life. Unlike my last visit here, I now had no outward measure that I was precious.

A soft bell toll interrupted my musings. Slowly I strolled back up the slope toward the chapel. But my mind did not enter into the ten-minute service. I was relieved, too, as we filed into lunch directly afterward, that the rule of silence meant I was not expected to join in any polite conversation.

I chose a seat in the dining room from which I could gaze out over the garden. I felt that would raise my spirits. Nature seemed so uncluttered by any of the burdens which seemed to weigh me down.

I recalled one very vivid memory of being told that I was precious — not by words, but by tears. It was during the four-month crisis earlier in the year. A very dear friend, Jennie, had once again left her young baby in order to journey to be with me. She had known how ill I was and had wanted to show how much she cared.

The day she came was one of my worst. I was so distracted by the burning intensity of pain that I had lost my way around the all-too-familiar ward. I had lost control of bodily functions. The nurse summoned the doctor out of surgery to come to me because she knew I was going downhill. When he arrived, I was unable to respond to his questions. I just stared through him, as indeed I did at Jennie when she arrived later.

It was a time when I was giving up my desire to live, my drive to get well. The doctor, I was later told, was himself distraught about my condition, probably because he knew that no medical man can stop a patient from giving up. He recognized how I felt. He described me as being "on a downward spiral." He knew that I could bear little more. I was utterly spent. That day, I was simply giving up.

Jennie did not try to cajole me out of my mood with philosophical reasons to live. She simply wept. She must have sensed immediately how I was and how I felt, for even as she took her coat off her face dissolved in tears. She dragged the nearest chair to be close beside me, took my unresponsive hand in both of hers, and sobbed. She buried her face in her hands and mine, kissing mine and stroking them as if she were handling a valuable treasure. Though I was passive, she made me feel precious.

I thank God that Jennie cried as she did. Some people would have suppressed their natural reaction, trying not to add to my problems by revealing their distress. But Jennie brought me into a sudden awareness of my situation. At the simplest level, she was so much herself that she was the first person whom I recognized that day. She brought me out of my stupor.

But she did more than that. Her tears showed me she cared. She caused the first stirrings in me to turn back from my only desire at that moment, which was to avoid more pain. Jennie could see that I had given up fighting, and clearly she longed to see me retrieve some spark of life. She valued me here. By her tears, she told me that my life *was* worthwhile.

Now, as I dined in silence, this memory was both consoling and upsetting. I was consoled to think of Jennie's indisputable love; yet I was perturbed to find that I almost wanted to repeat the whole scene so that I could feel reassured thus again.

Watching a squirrel darting up a tree outside, I felt I was beginning to understand why I was not particularly thankful to have been saved from dying in the hospital. The trouble was, I did not really believe that I was precious — precious to God, precious in the world.

Stripped of all worldly reassurance that I was making a valuable contribution to life, I had lost my sense of self-worth. The spiritual lessons I thought I had learned from Mo's poem were merely head knowledge and not a heartfelt conviction. God's words of comfort did not really encourage me. I had lost touch with the truth and reality of His pronouncement: "You are precious in my eyes, and honored, and I love you." I reacted by saying to God in a rather embarrassed way, "Gosh; that's nice of You." But I did not feel any different.

I glanced across at Matthew, who was eating awkwardly from his wooden bowl. What was he thinking, I wondered. He, more than anyone else, was caught up in the cost of my being alive; he was the one who supported me so strongly throughout both the crises and the long-term, residual pain. Yet he had never once suggested that the value of my life was not worth the pain, even though he too was caught up in that cost. He did not feel, as I did, that my life was just a burden.

My eyes filled with tears as I thought once again of the burden I felt myself to be: a burden to myself, enduring pain and feeling unwell, and a burden to others who had to endure my limitations and my moans.

Suddenly I was aware of Sister Rachel looking at me. I had been so lost in thought that I had forgotten that I was among others.

There was a gentle knock on the door of my room late in the afternoon. I knew then that Sister Rachel had noticed the signs of my low spirits. She sat on my bed as she asked how I was.

"I don't know," was my lame reply. "I just don't know." I was too bewildered to be objective about myself.

"You've been through a great ordeal," she said with conviction. "A lot has happened to you physically. You need time to catch up emotionally and spiritually."

I smiled and relaxed a little. It was an enormous relief to be accepted so fully. Sister Rachel was very perceptive and wise. I felt able to trust her with what was weighing so heavily on my heart.

"I know I ought to be grateful to God for healing me," I began tentatively. "But I just don't feel glad to be alive."

"Like a death wish, you mean?" Sister Rachel frowned a little.

"No. I don't actively want to die. I'm feeling much more passive than that. I just lack any enthusiasm for living."

"But you've been profoundly weakened, Jane. Not just physically, but in every way. Anyone is bound to feel this after being as ill as you have been, quite apart from the pain you're still having to combat every day. You're a strong person. You expect yourself to dance through everything, but you are setting goals which are too high." Her eyes twinkled affectionately.

Comforted a little by her reassurance, I dared to explain further.

"It's not just that, though. This morning I realized that I don't feel I'm special." I could not say more, for fear that my voice might betray how close I was to breaking down.

"Aren't you allowing yourself to forget all the signs from other people who have shown you how special you are to them? You yourself have written that to me in your letters."

She was right. People had reached out to me in many different ways: from those who sent simple but caring messages by card or with flowers, to those who gave up whole weeks of their time to help run the house.

"Yes, that has helped. But it doesn't stop my underlying feeling that I am now thoroughly restricted in what I can do in life. I mean, it wouldn't really have mattered if I were not in the world. If I had died when we expected me to—well, everyone would have been sad, but they would have got over it. Life would have gone on without me. So, is it important that I'm still here? What does it mean, 'You are precious'?"

I looked at her doubtfully, but her bowed head signaled that she was ready to listen to more.

"Because as far as I am concerned, it means telling myself, 'Keep going, Jane. God says it's worth your being alive so you must trust Him. Keep battling through pain. Try to endure suffering patiently.' But it's hard . . . it's so hard . . . " And my voice trailed away.

There was a silence between us, but I knew that Sister Rachel was not uncomfortable. The serenity in her face encouraged me to open up more fully.

"The trouble is, I suppose, that I allow my self-esteem to be either built up or eroded by other people's images of me. I work my guts out trying to be noticed as doing well, be it at work or among friends or in the church fellowship. I enjoy giving of myself because it is fruitful — it gives me the feedback that my role in life is appreciated according to what I give. Being appreciated makes me feel precious."

Sister Rachel nodded with understanding. She knew about dying to self. Part of her vocation had been to learn death to her own desires and ambitions through the three promises she had made as a nun.

"This illness has forced me into a place where I am restrained from giving as I would like to. I am forced instead to receive. You mentioned just now about all the care I've been shown. Perhaps people think I must feel precious because I receive so much kindness from those who want to minister to me. But I'm so accustomed to 'earning' my feeling of being precious that I find it difficult to stop giving and simply, passively, to receive."

Already I was feeling better for talking all this out. I could almost guess her "answer" before Sister Rachel spoke.

"But our Lord does not think of importance and value as we do. He wants us to learn that we are precious to Him in whatever state we are in. He values us for who we are in the quietness of our soul."

I was silenced, at last, by the wisdom of her words. Then, before leaving me to rest once more, Sister Rachel asked me to think about a verse. I knew it well. Psalm 46, verse 10: "Be still, and know that I am God."

"Spend time with it," she said confidently. "It may help you now."

I thought at first that it was an obvious verse for her to quote to me. What else was I doing at the retreat other than being still? Yet I admired Sister Rachel greatly, and I knew that after her years of close pilgrimage with her Lord, anything she said was worth taking seriously.

9. Refined by Fire

*Your faith — of greater worth than gold,
which perishes even though refined by fire —
may be proved genuine and may result in praise,
glory and honor when Jesus Christ is revealed
(1 Peter 1:7).*

For the rest of the day at the retreat, I held the verse in mind: "Be still . . . and know that I am God." I meditated on those words while brushing my teeth, eating my meals, kneeling quietly before the cross in the little chapel. The next day in my reading I came across some words in Latin: *Vacate et videte* — "Make empty and see."

I gazed pensively at the huge log fire beside me.

So, I told myself, *this is the key. I must empty out all the things which lead to my self-satisfaction, and come to God with nothing. He's not interested in my achievements. He wants only me, in my emptiness. Only then can He do what He wills in me.*

During the following several months I kept these thoughts uppermost in my mind. I found myself much less despondent whenever I was faced with the limitations set by the continuing low-level pain. Then, at Christmastime, another dear friend confirmed my thoughts about "doing" vs. "being." Sally wrote in her Christmas letter:

> In writing this letter about the "doings" of the year, one is tremendously aware that these are only the icing on the cake, and that the all-important work is that of the Spirit of God working within our lives.

As I look back, I know that the Spirit of God, working within me, had taken away much of my "doing." He has worked like a gardener pruning a valuable plant or tree, in that He has not merely cut out dead or useless growth, He has also cut me where I have been fruitful and growing healthily. This is exactly what Jesus said: "Every branch that does bear fruit he prunes, that it may bear more fruit" (John 15:2).

To find areas of my life being cut out by God has sometimes been hard. At times I've felt that He is so ruthless in His pruning, and it hurts so much, that I could not possibly be precious to Him. But I know that is not true. Again, it is through a poem that I have been able to see beyond the hurt of what God has taken away from me, and to trust that He has a loving purpose:

> It is the branch that bears the fruit
> that feels the knife
> To prune it for a larger growth,
> a fuller life . . .
>
> It is the hand of Love Divine
> that holds the knife,
> That cuts and breaks with tenderest touch,
> That thou, whose life has borne some fruit
> May'st now bear much.

Whatever pain my Father has asked me to endure is not worthless or without a loving purpose—however unloving it seems at times. I should not be surprised, nor should my faith waver, when some fruitful area of my life is cut away. But that is easier for me to write about than to endure. No amount of acceptance diminishes the dreadful reality of suffering.

Sometimes it is hard to discern when the Spirit of God is at work, and where His enemy is endeavoring to destroy. They may both want to cut away fruitful areas of my life, but for very different reasons. My Father only takes something away in order to make room for even fuller growth. His enemy would want me to become bitter, resentful and self-pitying.

I have needed to trust my Father never to cut anything out of my life except with loving hands which tend the wounds where He has pruned. His purpose is never to destroy because, He says clearly, "You are precious." I know He cares for me even when I do not really feel the tenderness of His love.

The practical outworking of the Spirit of God working within our lives can seem very, very, hard. I have often sung the song:

> Spirit of the living God
> Fall afresh on me . . .
> Break me, melt me
> Mold me, fill me.

God has answered, and He continues to answer, that prayer. He has broken me, and when I have felt the pain of being broken I have reflected on how much easier it is to sing the song than to accept the brokenness.

God has used physical suffering to break me. There are many little reminders in day-to-day life which cause me to think of my body's brokenness and incompleteness. When I see the scars from twelve abdominal operations, I am reminded that my physical brokenness also represents a brokenness of my spirit. Through physical surgery, God has "opened me up" and shown me parts of myself which I may have preferred not to see. But He has done it in order to remold me.

The smallest little thing occasionally reminds me that part of my womanhood has been taken away. Whenever I see the sales machines in ladies' restrooms, for example, I feel slightly less of a woman. I know I should count my blessings and I am glad to be free from the woman's monthly complaints, but I also feel left out, incomplete, broken.

God calls all of us to be broken, just as He was broken. In the upper room, Jesus took a whole loaf of bread and broke it into pieces as a dramatic illustration of what was to happen to His body. He asked His disciples, and He asks us, to follow Him.

God has melted me. I probably would have welcomed a pleasantly gentle heat to make me aglow with His Spirit, that would not have been hot enough to melt me. Instead, He has put me through a great burning intensity of heat, just as gold has to be put into a white-hot furnace in order to be melted. The fire of purification has felt so hot, so painful, that I have often wondered why I ever asked God to melt me. Yet I know that God has only done this because He values me so much. He is so interested in the quality of my life that He purifies me in the fire—because I am precious.

Looking back, I can see clearly that God has melted away a lot of rubbish from my life, and that however unbearable, His fire has strengthened my faith just as Peter wrote: "Your faith [is] more precious than gold which though perishable is tested by fire" (1 Peter 1:7).

God is molding me, and in being molded I have had to learn to be pliable so He can reshape me as He wants. He keeps on and on, just as a potter persists at his clay. I know that with each successive bout of illness I change a little, as God knocks off another sharp edge from me, but sometimes I feel tired and dizzy going round the potter's wheel. I look at those who do not seem to be having such a hard time, and fall into the trap of self-pity.

Yet I do know that God does not delight in causing His little ones to suffer. He continues to mold me because He is delighted to create vessels according to His design. I am beginning to learn not to wish that I could jump off the wheel, but to give myself more to His hands. I am beginning to pray honestly, "Lord, keep turning your wheel today, so that Your hands can mold me as You desire."

Being broken, melted and molded leaves a vessel which is ready to be filled. My value in life to Him lies *in my emptiness*. I can only be filled by Him when I make space for Him, which means emptying myself. The Holy Spirit has had the hard work of breaking my strong exterior, melting me to the core and molding me. All His work, which continues, has been in order to fill me.

God has filled me, quietly and undramatically. I know that at times I would have preferred to remain filled than to dare to pray, again and again, for the hurt of being broken, melted and molded. But God yearns for me to keep growing, to keep being filled. He wants to keep working in me because I am precious.

I constantly need to keep readjusting my perspectives. So much of what I see around me threatens to deceive me with the lie that it is a person's achievements that give him value. Consequently I begin to fear that the debilitating aspects of my suffering rob me of my worth. But God views things differently. He loves me for who I am more than for what I can do. And if it was my very pain that forced me into discovering this deep and vital truth, then surely I should embrace it rather than despise it.

10. Be Healed

*He said to her, "Daughter, your faith
has healed you. Go in peace
and be freed from your suffering"*
(Mark 5:34)

It was a great relief and release to my spirit when I began to build my life on the rock of God's love for me, regardless of what I could produce for Him. But I could not allow that to lull me into a totally passive attitude toward life. I know God is able to take away all pain. I have seen His power at work in others, and of course I have read about His miracles while His Son was on earth. Couldn't He decide to intervene in my suffering and use His great healing power to put an end to all my pain?

Once someone told me very clearly, "You must thank God that He has already healed you." I looked up from my prone position on the floor. A man was crouching down near my head. It was he who had caught me as I dropped. He had overheard the prayer for my healing and was, it seemed, adding the final touches to the prayer.

A man who was well known for the powerful gift of healing which God had given to him was leading the meeting. Four of us had gone to Matlock to see and hear him, and possibly to seek ministry through the laying on of hands.

I had hesitated about attending. I knew, partly, that I would be going for the wrong reasons — I was intrigued to see this man and witness some of the famous signs and wonders associated with his ministry. *But then, I consoled myself, a lot of people came to Jesus for the wrong reasons, such as curiosity, while He was on the earth. But Jesus never turned them away. Likewise, God will accept me if I am truly drawing near to Him for whatever initial reason I go.*

But this was only a small part of my hesitancy. There was much more than that, something which went much deeper. The trouble was, I had gone to these meetings before — I was almost embarrassed to recall how often. I had experienced the laying on of hands so many times, by so many people. I had been prayed over and anointed with oil by countless men of God. Was it right for me to go yet again? Was I seeking something magical in this man? Because if so, was I not in danger of worshipping the man, rather than God himself?

Had God not heard me the first time? By asking for the same thing each time, was I actually evading God's response? I had an uncomfortable inkling that maybe He could have been trying hard to give me an answer, that He had some purpose in withholding physical healing.

If I went that evening, wasn't I just trying yet another key in the lock? As if healing were like a gift in a locked cupboard, available only to those who had the right key. But that seemed to contradict how I thought of God. I did not think it was in His nature to withhold something good just because I did not pray in the "right" way with the "right" words. After all, Jesus had despised the Pharisee's "right" form of prayer and had honored the genuineness of the tax-collector's simple, humble prayer: "God, be merciful to me — a sinner!" (Luke 18:13)

I laid aside all these questions, and more. I had been persuaded to go. I must have been desperate. At any cost, I wanted to be completely free of pain. Physical pain lingered on even though the crisis in 1980 was now over and I had recently returned to work. Mentally I was still in pain, too, fighting against the terrifying memories of the severe physical symptoms I had had to endure. And emotionally it was a struggle to resume my enthusiastic work as a midwife after my own hysterectomy. I had chosen to do so; I wanted to overcome; I was determined not to be defeated by it — but it was still a struggle.

"Just think what you might be missing," said Alastair and Alison as they urged me to accompany them to the healing service. "Swallow your pride and come on."

The idea that it might be sheer pride which was stopping me from drawing near to God was the last straw. Dragging Matthew along with us, we all jumped into the car together.

I did not realize how much God had taught me in this healing service, and the countless others, until later when Matthew began his ministry as a pastor in Beverley. During our four years there, I came to know a lively girl named Carol. She was a teacher who was full of character and laughter. At twenty-five years old she was only a little younger than myself. Then, two days after we first met, she was diagnosed as having multiple sclerosis.

Carol was shattered. Such a diagnosis was to affect her whole way of living and she was asking some heart-searching questions. Suddenly we had a lot in common. Very early in our friendship our conversations were deep and brutally honest.

One evening we sat together at a church meeting. I noticed that Carol lacked her usual sparkle and her eyes seemed distant and sad.

"How are you?" I asked, but not until I was putting my coat on, ready to leave.

"Fine, thanks."

I knew that answer very well. I had used it countless times myself.

"Rubbish!" I retorted, but with a smile. Carol looked up at me and broke into laughter at herself. She enjoyed being teased like a normal person, instead of constantly pitied about her health. Her face softened with relief that she had been understood a little without needing to go through the wearisome task of explaining her complex feelings to me.

"It *is* rubbish, I know," she said at last. "I've wanted so much to talk to you. I've even tried writing to you several times, but each time the letter has ended up in the waste basket."

I sat down again beside her. I did not mind if we were the last people to leave the meeting—Carol needed to talk. I knew how hard I had found it to pull down my cheerful facade of saying I was "fine, thanks." This was the first time Carol had begun to be truly honest and open with me and I did not want to let her down.

"Is the MS itself getting you down?" I asked.

Carol shook her head. "Well, partly, I suppose. The symptoms are getting worse. I can't see properly now—everything has a double image so I keep crashing into doors or walls, thinking they are in a different place from where they actually are. And I'm also having 'accidents' sometimes and I have to wear pads, but waterproof underpants make a rustling noise which is awful. Not the sort of thing to help one make friends quickly. I get the most amazing looks from some folk, you know."

I sensed that underneath her apparent lightheartedness Carol was feeling very low. There was nothing I could say. No solution, no answer. Just, "I'm sorry." At least she knew I meant it.

My sincerity helped Carol to trust me a little further. "The thing is, while I'm acquiring these 'extra' problems related to the MS, everyone I love and trust seems to be convinced that I will be healed, and soon. I feel I'm under immense pressure."

"Pressure from others, you mean?"

"Mmmm. Almost unbearable at times." Carol looked away pensively before continuing, "Don't get me wrong—it would be lovely and I would be a fool not to ask God for healing and expect it."

Carol and I had both witnessed recently the quiet miracle of David, a twenty-year-old man in our church whose crippling arthritis had been healed. Neither of us had any doubts that God does heal today. Yet Carol's experience in her own suffering happened to be different. She explained, "Last time I was at a healing service it was particularly difficult for me. I felt everyone in the room was expecting me to be healed, and if I wasn't, then the fault could only be mine."

"How can people say that?" I muttered, more to myself than to Carol. The question was rhetorical but Carol answered nevertheless.

"Oh, Jane, you know perfectly well how their argument goes: that God wants to heal, He wants His children to be healthy, and we have only to ask."

"Yes, I've had all that said to me," I replied. I was almost tired of hearing it. "Quite honestly, I often get the feeling that it's easier for people to say that than to go a bit deeper. They can remain untouched by the pain of long-term suffering if they can give a quick solution to it."

"But how do you cope with people who try to help like this? Are they right? Oh, I'm so confused."

I thought for a moment. It perturbed me to see that Carol had been upset, especially by those who tried to help. I had experienced similar confusion myself and could have said so much to Carol I hardly knew where to start. There was no simple answer.

I began gently. "Well, it didn't take long for me to realize that it isn't always as simple as some people suggest. If, as you say, we 'only have to ask,' then without a doubt I would have been healed a long time ago. But I wasn't."

Carol answered quickly. "No, it's not exactly straightforward. You have to have faith, don't you? People say that it's my lack of faith that's stopping me from being healed."

I felt my anger rising. I find it very hard to remain patient when people give such a glib explanation as that.

"How much faith do they think you need?" I asked quickly. "Because if you look in the Bible, Jesus said all you need is faith the size of a grain of mustard seed. That's enough to move a mountain. Some Christians can make you feel utterly condemned if your faith isn't the size of a melon! But that's other people, not God. A mustard seed is enough for God. Have you got that much faith?"

Carol giggled. "Yes, I have!" She seemed pleased to have some assurance that she was not so completely feeble a Christian as she had been made to feel, at least not on that score.

"In any case," I continued, "people who say your healing depends on you having enough faith should read Hebrews. In among the long list of heroes who are examples of those with faith, there's a little verse . . . " I fumbled to find Hebrews, chapter 11. "It says, 'And all these, though well attested by their faith, did not receive what was promised, since God had foreseen something better for us'" (Hebrews 11:39). I looked at Carol, whose forehead was puckering.

"What on earth does that mean?" she asked.

"It means we can be sure that if we fail to receive what God has promised, like healing, we can take heart. He has something better for us. Pressing on *without* receiving is actually commended. According to the person who wrote Hebrews, it is evidence of faith."

Carol sighed ruefully. "Oh, it would be nice if things were really like that."

"I think it *is* that way—when God chooses it to be." I became quiet before adding, "I have to believe that."

"Anyway," my voice became a little harder, "if they are so impressed about the need for faith, you should remind them about Jairus's daughter, or the centurion's servant. It was the faith of the friends, and not the sufferer's faith, which impressed Jesus."

Carol obviously could not detach herself enough from the pressure of her friends to be as frivolous as I was. She went on, "They tell me adamantly that I will be fully fit very soon."

My cheeks flushed as I saw how people sometimes manage to avoid facing up to suffering. How much easier it was to say that Carol would be healed, than to think she might not be! She was so bright and vivacious—how could God let her become crippled? Perhaps, also, I lost my patience because I felt trapped by being forced to face up to suffering and pain. Maybe I wished that I, too, could have explained it away so easily.

I burst out, "How can they be adamant? Have they asked God? Do they know the mind of Christ? Usually those who genuinely do have His mind are humble, not adamant. Have they given time to listen to God—specifically about you and your MS? How, exactly, did it come to them that this is God's will for you?"

I could have gone on, but the glint in Carol's eye helped me laugh at my forthrightness, despite the fact that I meant every word I had said.

"You often talk about seeking God's will," Carol prompted me.

"Yes, I do. It's something which I learned a lot about while staying at a retreat. There I discovered that prayer is not telling God what you want, but opening yourself up to what He wants in you. For me, that takes much more faith. For you, and your adamant friends, it means spending time silently, seeking His will. I think the only time we 'just have to ask' for healing is when we know God's will for each particular person."

Carol nodded thoughtfully. "But according to them, I'm not the one to know God's will. You see, you've just reminded me. They say that my lack of faith creates a wall between me and my MS, and God and His healing."

I sighed inwardly at the effect of such advice on someone like Carol, whose pain made her so vulnerable.

"You *have* been confused, haven't you?"

Carol's eyes moistened. I so much wanted to comfort her, to assure her of how graciously God accepted her even when others seemed only to find faults.

"Listen. No words or arguments can help when anyone's feeling as you are now. Only you and God know if there's a wall between you. Don't rely on me or on anybody else. Just trust your own relationship with God. Why don't you go home now—it's getting late anyway—but go back and find peace on your own with Him. Try to look at Him and be aware of Him looking at you. You will know if there is a wall between you. And if there isn't, take courage not to let others make you feel guilty."

Carol nodded, sniffing back her tears. "Yes, that will help," she conceded, reaching for her coat.

As we walked toward the door I thought out loud, "The old devil would be thrilled if he could get at you. He knows it's hard for you to reject what loved ones say. Only, sometimes, you must."

11. *My Ways Are Not Your Ways*

*For my thoughts are not your thoughts,
neither are your ways my ways
(Isaiah 55:8).*

I went home in a pensive mood. That night it was hard to sleep. It was all very well for me to have talked to Carol as I had, but I remembered times when I had felt hurt as she was now. Deeply hurt. I thought of how often I had found myself alone after visitors had left me, feeling as if it were my own fault that I was not better. People may have meant kindly, but I'm sure they could not have realized how devastated I was by some of their advice.

The sorts of things they said went round and round my head as I tossed and turned in bed.

"I've just been reading Matthew's gospel where Jesus says, 'Ask and you will receive.' " (How often I had heard that!) "Well presumably, Jane, you can't have asked Him properly."

Not asked—pleaded! Besought. Hammered at His door. Wept. Cried out. Thrown myself at His feet. If He hadn't heard me, He was not the God I knew I could trust.

I remembered, with some measure of shame, an occasion when Mike had got in touch with me. He did not know me at all well, but he had heard of my illness at his church. Having prayed for me, he wanted to do something tangible to help. He decided to visit me at home.

I found the time with him very tense. None of his helpful suggestions were new to me, though he was clearly enthusiastic about each one. Unfortunately—and this was where I felt somewhat ashamed as I recalled the scene—I did not have the mental energy to be more than blunt in my replies.

"You should pray in Jesus' name."

"I always do."

"Why don't you call together the elders of the church for laying on of hands, as in James 5?"

"I have. Lots of times."

"You should be anointed with oil."

"I have been."

"You need to find out if there's something in your past which is preventing you from being healed."

"I went with Matthew to a friend who is a Christian psychiatrist, in order to pursue that one. After a couple of sessions, she asked to stop because she felt I was too normal to have anything major causing problems."

"You ought to go to such-and-such a man. He has a healing ministry."

"I went last year."

Mike's mind was fixed on physical healing. I was trying to force him to realize that there was an alternative to the way in which he was talking. I wanted to make him see that no one formula had "worked." I had done all the things he was suggesting, and was still left in pain.

Finally he sighed, exhausted. "Then you must have been healed. You should thank God."

At that point in the conversation my hands were clutching a hot water bottle under the quilt, as I tried to find something to soothe the pain searing through me. There had been a time, years before, when I would have wondered if it were just my imagination that I was still in great pain when someone was telling me that I had been healed. But not this time.

Mike was so quick with one suggestion after another that I found myself responding defensively. I wanted to shut him up, which I knew was less than gracious of me. I felt so strongly that he was barging in on a delicate subject, that I did not want to give him my time. Yet in the end God's graciousness prevailed and I tried to explain a little.

"My first reaction to this pain continuing on and on was like yours now," I told him, trying not to sound too patronizing. "I thought praying for healing was something I must do correctly in order to get what I wanted. Healing seemed right. I found that when I was clearly 'failing' — or apparently failing — I began to think in a completely different way about prayer."

Mike looked at me suspiciously. I prayed silently to the Lord to give me patience and honesty.

"When I pray now, I concentrate very much less on *what* I am actually asking for. I am sure He wants me to seek more of *who* He is. Once I have that in perspective, He can reveal to me the specific things He wants me to pray about."

Mike's face furrowed. I was risking a lot by trying to explain myself. I was laying myself open to accusations or criticism about my own pilgrimage with the Lord. Could he understand me, I wondered. I knew that my prayer life was a personal matter and I should not mind what anyone else thought about it, but even so I did not want Mike to be scornful of my attitude toward it.

I tried to explain myself more clearly. "One of the nuns at a convent I once visited put it much better than I can. She said, "Prayer is not an easy way of getting God to do things for you, but a difficult way of allowing Him to do things in you.""

"Isn't that just playing with words?" asked Mike. "What's the difference?"

"The difference is in the answer we seek. The 'answer' to prayer is not in receiving a gift, but in meeting the Giver."

I realized I was trying to condense into one conversation all that God had been teaching me over many years. Healing was an enormous subject, of which prayer was only one part. I tried to put very simply what was uppermost in my mind.

"I believe God wants the best for us, always."

"Right."

"My idea of the best is healing."

"Right."

"But God has withheld that, despite my asking for it in all the ways I have told you. Now, I could blame myself for lacking faith or somehow not asking in the right way. But I know I have asked in every way I can, and not alone but with the support of many faithful Christians."

"Yes?" Mike was not quite sure he could trust me. Again, I uttered a silent prayer to ask the Lord to help me be true to Him and not concerned about what Mike thought of me.

"Or I could blame God, saying either that He has not heard me or that He is mean, withholding something good. But I cannot do either of those things, because deep down I trust Him. I just know that He does not delight in making His children suffer."

I had to show Mike that I was genuine. I had sounded so negative when he had first arrived that He might have thought I was dismissive of God. He would have been so wrong. I know God always wants to do more for me and in me than I can ever imagine.

"So it must be something else." I paused. I did not want to say what was so important to me if Mike was not listening properly.

"What?" he asked, interested. It had never occurred to him that, unlike us, God Himself might actually have wanted something other than physical healing for me at that point. "I can only conclude that He has not healed me because He has something *better* for me. As I said before, my idea of the best is healing. But for the moment anyway, it seems that's not God's idea of the best. He does say, "My ways are not your ways." Although this dreadful pain is not my way, or the way I would choose, it's obviously His."

"That's very harsh, isn't it?" At least Mike was thinking about what I had said.

"No. It seems harsh and it feels harsh, but I stake everything on my faith that God is not harsh. And I have been encouraged in many ways."

I told Mike of one example of encouragement. I had heard by letter that, while praying for me, a man named Peter had had a picture in his mind. He could see the face of Christ, who was looking upon me in my suffering. Peter had been surprised that, instead of encountering pain and confusion, there had been great joy and light. Jesus was looking with desire and love upon what He saw forming and coming out of the pain. Though He was mindful of the pain, the Lord took delight in the very thing which I found hard. That encouraged me to see my suffering more from His viewpoint. It helped me to share some of His joy.

"How could God ever *want* pain?" Mike was very puzzled.

"Oh, I don't know," I sighed. "I haven't got all the answers. I cannot explain God. I can only tell you of my own experience. Every time I have gone forward for laying on of hands for healing, the pain has become much worse. But alongside this I have experienced a huge injection of spiritual closeness to the Lord. It's as if God takes me, lifts me up and reassures me that He is doing with me just what He wills."

"And so you really thank Him for that?" Mike was pressing me very hard for realistic answers.

I paused. "Sometimes." I hugged the hot water bottle more closely to myself. "I wish I could honestly say always. If I had been healed physically, I'd have leapt up and said, 'Thank you, Lord!' Well, just because I can't always see the areas which He is healing, shouldn't I still be thanking Him? I suspect that His healing in me is much deeper than anything physical."

Mike's eyes sparkled for a second; he almost spoke but then stopped himself.

"What is it?" I asked. I was still unsure of him.

"Well . . . it's just that you reminded me of the story of the ten lepers. They were all healed, physically. Yet nine out of ten of them danced off without even speaking to Jesus again—not even to thank Him. It seems to me—and I know I'm only an onlooker—but, well, it's quite a miracle that you've at least kept coming to Him."

I lay back on the pillows and smiled. I no longer felt accused. At last Mike and I were communicating, rather than fighting against one another. He had understood – at least a little. He had recognized that my suffering was a vehicle for faithfulness and trust in the Lord; he saw that it was not necessarily proof of my faithlessness. The relief of that was a positive encouragement to me.

What I had been trying to share with him was the acceptance to which God had brought me after the terrible crisis at Tina's flat. I had only talked about it so directly once before, and that was to Graham. Sitting in Colin's house, waiting to go back into the hospital and not knowing how long I would even live, Graham had asked me, "Do you feel God is ignoring your pain, or that He is letting things get out of hand?"

"No." I was sure of my answer despite the desperate anguish I felt. "No, I don't. I may not like what He's doing, I may disagree with Him, but I've put myself in His hands and asked Him to do the best for me. I know He can heal me. But He hasn't, yet. I can trust His wisdom. While I loathe the pain itself, I refuse to be tempted to mistrust Him. He knows best. Having asked Him to do His will, I can only trust Him that what's happening to me now *is* His will."

"How are you so sure?" Graham had asked me. I replied honestly, "Because God is in it. It's accompanied by such peace, such an assurance of Him with me that I know it's not His mistake."

This was my conviction, my healing. To abandon myself completely into His hands, no matter what pain that caused in me, allowing Him to perform a deep and thorough healing. To follow Him obediently – even to the furnace for Him to purify me; to the garden for Him to prune me, cutting back good growth and making room for even more;

to the threshing-mill for Him to thrash out the wheat from the chaff.

At the healing service in Matlock, the man leaning over me had said, "You must thank God that He has already healed you." Maybe he was right. But I have found that whenever I consider the kind of healing which I imagine that man meant—a freedom from all pain—I encounter problems and questions. I start to turn away from the depths of healing which God has wrought in me. I begin to resent the pain of humility, and my trust gives way to confusion and bewilderment. God's healing is so much bigger, broader and more creative than man's limited ideas of pain-free solutions.

For me, to be healed was to be taken more deeply into God, to plumb more fully the mystery of His power and love. To lose sight of that would be to lose sight of my Lord and to be cast into the desolation of crying, "My God, my God, why hast thou forsaken me?" (Matthew 27:46).

12. Why Hast Thou Forsaken Me?

My God, my God, why have you forsaken me?
Why are you so far
from the words of my groaning?
(Psalm 22:1)

If I wanted to be "healed," I had concluded, then I wanted above everything to find and possess more of God. That meant not only knowing Christ in the power of His resurrection, but also in the fellowship of His sufferings — becoming like Him in His death (see Philippians 3:10-11).

Resuming a normal life after a long period of illness has always signified far more to me than merely the end of convalescence. My return to work in September 1980 found me constantly trying to balance the story of my pain with that of my successes.

As soon as I was back, I was confronted again by my "successes" in midwifery. I was popular among the patients and sought after by the doctors. Patients did not hide their disappointment that they had not had me to look after them throughout their pregnancy and labor, and many of the staff shared openly their relief that "at last things will be done properly again!"

It did not stop there. While I had been off work, a simple audio-visual program which I had compiled had begun to be used in other hospitals around Britain. It was praised enthusiastically by other midwives, and before long I was flown down to London to receive a national award. During that trip I was commissioned to create five new films which were to be distributed around the world.

I was positively exhilarated. I had known utter brokenness in my pain, but now I was being reminded that it was part of God's plan for me to know great fulfillment. Soon I was lecturing to other health professionals, first in Britain and then internationally — as far afield as Australia. Once again, I was able to enjoy the glow of achievement and satisfaction, perhaps all the more so because now I saw it in a clearer perspective.

When others looked at me, they saw a strong person. I was considered the character of the department, well known for being able to combine efficiency with good fun. Most of the time I felt confident, even elated, that things were going so well.

And yet . . . what of the pain? How did that find its place in the life of one for whom everything was going so well in so many areas? Not least among these happy events was the news that we could expect our first baby by adoption. Should we have seen things as many of our friends did — that all this apparent "success" was some form of compensation from on High for my pain? Was the adoption of Angus — and three years later, Philippa — that joyful beginning of what has continued to be a most wonderful gift to us? Was that the icing on the cake to make up for everything?

If this is so, then my emotions have not been guided by reason. For there have been times — there still are — when I feel that no amount of good things can ever counterbalance the utter brokenness within me. I still feel weak, vulnerable, torn apart by pain or the memories of it. Whenever such hurt within me surfaces, I subconsciously long for this part of me to be understood, loved, comforted.

Often, not even aware of what I am searching for deep within my soul, I do not find what my heart has craved. I fail to ask for help. Those who may have seen only my "successes" have not realized my unspoken needs. And so all too easily, times develop when I feel forsaken not only by others but — because they are the Lord's ambassadors — by God himself.

I remember one such occasion very well. Lying down to rest alone one afternoon, I was suddenly aware of the hurt, confusion and loneliness which filled my mind and soul.

I had been invited to lecture at another world congress on nursing. I had hesitated in accepting, for I had been away from clinical work for two years since Angus's birth. Nevertheless, the invitation had seemed genuine so, encouraged by Matthew, I eventually accepted and began to look forward to the stimulation and challenge. The three days away from home were bound to be busy, but we knew I would benefit from the break and the luxury of being looked after in an expensive hotel.

Outwardly, everything was going very well. During my first lecture the previous day I had felt inspired, and the hundreds of nurses and health visitors listening had responded enthusiastically. At one point they had burst into spontaneous applause and laughter, quickly melting my nervousness in front of so many professionals. I knew I could look forward to leading a workshop the following morning with fresh confidence.

Back in my plush hotel room that evening, I reveled in the comfort of it all. A phone call home had given me the opportunity for a lovely chat with Matthew and with Angus, who had sounded very happy. "Did you see Princess Anne, Mommy?" was all he had wanted to know. I chuckled to myself as I lay soaking in a bath full of bubbles later that evening. As I committed the day to the Lord, I remembered a verse in Joel which someone had once thought very apt for me: "I will restore to you the years which the swarming locust has eaten" (Joel 2:25).

I had had years of being stripped of everything through my pain. But I had had much restored: my fulfillment now, my career, even a family against all the odds. I thanked the Lord for His many blessings to me and drifted off into a very contented sleep.

But the next morning I was suddenly plunged into distress. I had taken a long time to wake up completely. As often happens, the abdominal discomfort which had become "normal" for me had been incorporated into my dreams.

This time, my dream had taken me back to the occasion when I was first ill, in Edinburgh. Half-awake, half-dreaming, I felt as I had then—too limp to move my heavy body for myself. I was aware of my heavy breathing and my body position, completely limp on the bed. In the dream, I relived the time when my breathing had been labored because of illness, and my limp body had been placed in a similar stretched-out position by the nurses.

It was only the faintest stirring in me which strove toward consciousness: this time because I was still mostly asleep, but in Edinburgh it had been because of the severity of the peritonitis. Overtaken by pain, I had been completely passive—all except for this one tiny stirring in me which struggled, even against my own will, to fight its way to life.

Although the anguish was only a memory, it was so vivid that I felt as if the situation was actually repeating itself in reality. But in Edinburgh there had been consolation. I could recall now how I had been comforted. I had been visited by one of my nursing tutors, Elaine. She had drawn alongside and shown her compassion to me, even though at the time I was too weak to respond. Her caring hand had gently held my forearm. It was as simple as that.

Desperately now, I longed for a gentle caress. I was reliving the scene, but without her caring touch. I wanted so much to be able to open my eyes and be comforted. I wanted to see someone like Elaine, not only beside me physically but "with" me in understanding, as she had been. In my sleepiness the pain was so vivid and alive; but in my semi-consciousness I also knew there was no one to help. I felt forsaken.

For as long as I could, I kept my eyes tightly closed, trying at least to envision Elaine's care and grasp it to meet my present need. If I could not be comforted as I would have liked, then at least I could try to imagine it.

Eventually the dream faded until I could no longer hold onto it. It was just a memory. The vision of someone caring for me was just a fancy. I struggled to put it out of my mind.

All day, I felt very fragile. The pain was "only in my mind," I knew, but I could not shrug it off. It was as if I was still enduring it, and therefore still had to be comforted with the sort of comfort I had experienced in my dream. I had every kind of distraction, but inside I was still hurting. As always after a dream such as that, I had to force myself to do everything. I had a workshop to lead. I had to be competent, but deep down I was crying.

And of course, people saw no need to comfort me, for nobody saw the pain inside me. I felt very alone. In one sense I wanted it like that; I certainly did not want to be pitied or made a fuss of. I did not want to be told I had "done well, considering . . . " I wanted to be told straight, either that I had done well or badly. I wanted honesty.

Occasionally during the day I found myself close to tears, so crushed did I feel even by bearing the memory of all the pain I had gone through. At one moment I nearly cracked. I had been listening to another nurse lecturing about patients having a hysterectomy. It was especially pertinent to me anyway, and during the question time I had asked about counseling help for such women. Her face had been so kind as she looked to me and replied, that I hardly heard her words. *She has compassion,* I thought. *This is true comfort — just the love in her eyes.* I had to bite my lip to fight back the tears.

Don't be silly, I told myself. *You're not ill now; you don't need comforting like that.*

But pain is a peculiar thing. Psychologically it often lasts longer than the physical symptom. It will not go away with reasoning or bargaining. It is a silent guest which comes and goes as it pleases.

I tried to pray. "Lord, these memories of pain are troubling me. I feel so confused and unsettled. I yearn to be comforted. You understand better than anyone else, better even than I do. Please, You be the one to hold me and speak reassuringly to me. Let me see Your eyes, for I know they are full of compassion. Let me feel the tenderness of Your love which I know is there."

But it was as if He was not there. As if He had withdrawn. Even spiritually, I felt utterly forsaken.

None of the events of the day, nor of my life, could console me in the emptiness I felt. This was something going on at the core of my being: a child unable to see her beloved Father. It was God Himself who seemed distant. No eternal blessing could ever compensate for that. I was weighed down in my spirit, as if under a burden of affliction.

Outward achievements only served to lure me into self-satisfaction, which dragged me even further away from the child-like place of dependence where I wanted to be.

By the time my workshop was over, I was exhausted. As soon as the crowd of people asking questions had disappeared, I slipped back to my room in the adjoining hotel.

13. A Pathway Through the Mighty Waters

Your path led through the sea,
your way through the mighty waters,
though your footprints were not seen
(Psalm 77:19).

With relief I drank in the soothing quietness of the beautiful hotel room, so pleasant after the constant tiring buzz of noise and chatter at the conference. I locked the door firmly and flopped onto the bed.

Once again, as soon as I closed my eyes I was taken straight back to that scene in Edinburgh. I could not push out of my mind the memory of my profound illness and weakness. I recalled how I had been unable even to swallow. I could almost feel again the saliva dribbling from my mouth, down the side of my cheek and onto the shoulder of the unfeminine hospital gown draped around me.

I was disturbed by all this; distressed to relive such weakness and pain. Yet, in a way, I wanted to relive it. I wanted to imagine Elaine's care once again, to feast on that recollection until I had had my fill.

I was so torn! I knew that, in the end, I would never have my fill. There was an aching void within me which could fade with time but would never go away completely. Nine years had passed since I had been in the hospital in Edinburgh, but still it seemed as clear in my mind as if it had been only a week before. Seeking consolation was useless, especially on my own as I was. It made things worse when I tried, because I became so bowed down by the memory of the pain that I felt increasingly vulnerable and isolated, far from any comfort.

"Help me, Lord!" I sobbed. "Please help me." I buried my head in the soft pillow.

But God was silent. There was no "answer." No response. I felt no different spiritually, although it was a relief for me to let the tears flow at last after having to detach myself from all the emotions of the morning at the conference.

I fumbled for my Bible. I wanted to look toward God for help—but I felt let down by Him. I was in trouble; this was one of the times when I needed Him most of all. And this was the very time He had chosen to hide His face from me.

Hardly daring to think or speak resentfully toward Him, I instead allowed the psalmist to express my own bewildered questions:

Why are you so far away, O Lord?
Why do you hide yourself when we are in trouble?
(Psalm 10:1, GNB).

How much longer will you forget me, Lord? For ever? . . .
How long will sorrow fill my heart day and night?
(Psalm 13:1-2, GNB).

There was no doubt in my mind that God was with me. I can only think that He had given me this faith;

certainly I could take no credit for it myself. The frustration was knowing that my Lord, my Father, *was* . . . but in darkness.

He was not visible. He was not where I wanted Him. He had promised to hold my hand, to be with me always, but I could not feel Him. I knew by heart a verse in Psalm 77:

> Thy way was through the sea, thy path through the great waters; yet thy footprints were unseen (Psalm 77:19).

One reassurance to me, once I was a little calmer, was that I knew I was not alone in experiencing this darkness. I had read a little of the spiritual masters, who seemed not to be surprised at this phenomenon. It seemed to be a special calling—to know Him in darkness. Sister Rachel had been very encouraging to me on one point. It was because she was one of the rare people who truly seemed to identify with this forsakenness that I could respect her wisdom and remember very clearly what she had written:

> If you are going to go deeper into a "knowledge" of God, you will be drawn into the wilderness to teach you the real meaning of faith. God does withdraw the "knowledge" of His presence in the realms of feelings, and we have to learn that love is of the will and not the emotions, so that we will "love Him though He slay us."

However, there was one danger. I was aware that, while my heavenly Father could withdraw Himself in order to deepen my faith, it was also true that His enemy, Satan, could use the same circumstance to try to turn me away from Him. So, even in my pitiful state, I said aloud with great authority, "And if you, Satan, have anything to do with this, then you can just go away. You have no business taunting me. I am a child of God, my Father. In the name of the Lord Jesus, just go away!"

After that, I knew I must try to distract my wandering thoughts. My willpower was stretched to the limits, so strong was the temptation to indulge in flights of imagination. I turned toward the shining metal panel beside my bed and switched on the radio. The sound of pop music was just fading. A disc jockey started talking about the birth of a self-help group. He described how a couple had lost their baby. The doctors and nurses had been very kind, but all too soon formal help had diminished and their friends began to stop talking about their grief. Every form of help they had first received gradually stopped. But their need for care and comfort had continued.

"No amount of sympathy can stop *you* having to go through it," they had said. "We had an aching void which was just not filled. We formed this group to help both ourselves and others in a similar unhappy position."

The disc jockey added his own comments to this "moving story." Sloppy music played in the background as his deep voice said sentimentally, "You admire the courage of that couple, don't you, when you hear how they surmounted that kind of unhappiness." Then the jangle of the next record boomed out and coaxed us all into a carefree mood once again.

But they had had no choice!

I groaned into my pillow. It was not romantic or heroic as he had made it seem. He was deceived. He saw only the areas in which they had been brave, but that was only one part of them. There would be another part which was crying out with the pain of their loss and grief.

He had made that couple's courage sound so glorious, but it would not have felt like that to them. They had probably felt totally unable to surmount their pain, but, like me, how could they express their inability to do so? There is no option; no way out. Pain simply takes over its victim. It governs every move, almost like a machine which has been wound up and cannot stop until it has run its course. That couple would not want admiration. Oh, maybe that was nice—just as it had been nice for me to be admired sometimes. But no amount of admiration counterbalances the heart's deep pain. And I knew that, as on that particular day, what I wanted was not admiration, either for surmounting my pain or for my lecture—though that had its place. Deep down I wanted tender, loving care.

The attraction of my dream and my memory of Elaine's visit to me in Edinburgh was that I had been comforted in my weakness. I had not had to fight to prove to her that I was brave. What I treasured in my memory was not her admiration, but her compassion. She had comforted me in my passivity even before I had known she was beside me. For once, I had been "caught"—unable to strive to show my courage. It was an unusual situation for me. I do not normally lie back and enjoy being comforted in weakness. To do so would feel like an indulgence in wallowing.

I turned over in bed, becoming drowsy with the radio's soft music. At last I slept, managing some escape from the heaviness of some of my thoughts.

I awoke gently this time, and tried to refresh myself for the conference once again. Standing under the shower in the elaborate hotel bathroom, I glanced up. The huge tinted mirror along one wall reflected my figure. The scar down my abdomen seemed to glare back at me, prominent and red. At that moment I hated it, or rather, what it represented. I did not want to look. Quickly I wrapped my warm towel around me and began to dress.

Was I covering up the story of my pain? Did I "cope" by hiding and suppressing the hurt? A particular phrase was ringing in my head. So often I had heard people say, "I don't know how you cope so marvelously."

They are wrong. They take me for what I seem to be. I do not feel brave. I do not deserve admiration. Inside myself, I do not "cope marvelously." When I have acute bouts of pain I have to struggle every minute, every hour, against crying out with the pain.

Throughout the whole day at the conference, I told no one of my inner desolation. I could not. If I had dared, what could I have said? I could think of nothing specific that I could ask anyone to do to help. I knew I wanted only comfort — but how could I have asked for that? There was a tedious history behind the inner pain I felt. How could anyone have understood it all?

In many ways, I could see why people said that I coped marvelously. I usually made myself appear normal, just as I did on that day; and I enjoyed doing so. But I also realized that throwing myself into life as I did prevented many others from knowing my pain. If I ever dared to share with people how I felt deep down, they invariably responded by saying, "Jane, I never knew."

That's it. They never really know. Pain is one's own. Others cannot know it at all. Perhaps everyone is in pain, in their own pain, living in isolation from one another. As the couple on the radio had said, "Others may help you cope, but in the end it's *you* who must go through it."

But I was a Christian. I knew God cares; that He helps people through everything. I knew He was with me. How could I feel alone?

I had received so much, and I had been wonderfully supported and cared for by family and friends. Was I being ungrateful by feeling alone?

No. Matthew often assured me that he understood too well ever to accuse me of that. However close we were to one another, he was still on the sidelines. That, in a way, was the awful thing he had to bear: to watch, to care, but be unable to take the pain away.

It was a long time afterward that I talked this through with a very dear friend, Sarah. I was again very low with yet another episode of pain.

"I don't know what to say to you, Jane," she said helplessly. "I feel terribly impotent, so useless. But there's nothing I can do to help you."

"You have helped," I told her with conviction. "You always take time to listen to me, without making me feel I'm a pest to you; and you find some encouragement to share without sounding empty. You will remain someone whom I can always trust at least to try to understand."

It was true. One source of my heavy-heartedness was that I had met some Christians who had just shrugged their shoulders and said, "Ah, well, God knows best." They had wanted to cheer me up, I knew, by helping me look on the bright side. But that just served to make me feel even more depressed, because I was unable to ignore the pain and difficulties as they seemed to expect of me. That made the pain all the more lonely.

The loneliness of pain is perhaps its most excruciating aspect. It threatens to cut one off from others, and, worst of all, it makes one feel abandoned by God Himself.

My conversation with Sarah continued on into the evening. She too had personal struggles which she needed to talk about. Recently, in the midst of painful difficulties, she had found it particularly hard to hold on to her faith in the goodness of God. As we shared together in fellowship about the times when we had each reached rock-bottom, we began to see something very precious.

I considered how Jesus must have felt when Judas Iscariot left the other disciples to plot his act of betrayal. Paradoxically, in Christian experience, death is always the gateway to life. Embracing that truth, I felt able once again to endure with patience.

14. Endure With Patience

*If we are distressed, it is for your comfort,
which produces in you patient endurance
of the same suffering we suffer
(2 Corinthians 1:6).*

I believe that God has called me to trust Him in darkness, to keep holding His hand even through the pain. He wants me to endure all things with Him.

Unfortunately, I cannot simply disregard all the pain and turn my back on suffering. Pain is not an optional extra, like a handbag which I can forget I am carrying. I only find it possible to live to the full by accepting life to the full—and that includes the pain. It means accepting the pain as part of *me,* part of being me. It is a hard path.

There is a form of tiredness which those who are never ill do not know. Often I am too tired to read, too weary to knit because the weight of my arms is too great. When I first awake from sleep I do not feel rested. I am still aware of the energy involved even in lifting up my head to turn toward the clock. When the pain has been bad for some time, even breathing is tiring. Holding my arms and body together in its very existence feels too much. I am just too weary.

I wonder how long I will keep going in this sort of state, but somehow I am still here. I have to concentrate on making my muscles hold me upright (people must wonder why I do not concentrate well on a conversation at times like these). I feel as if I am on autopilot, forcing myself to walk, throwing one step after another. Time drags. I try to stop myself looking at the clock. But then suddenly I realize that more time has passed than I had guessed, and that seems a real blessing. I look forward to this painful phase of life being over.

But as "this phase" of life goes on and on, I realize that pain is an intregal part of my very living. I cannot continue to wait for life to pass, but I have to get down to living without watching the minutes ticking by. I cannot leave my pain at the cross because I could not walk away without it. Instead, I have to throw myself into making the most of living in pain.

Pain takes its toll both for me and, of course, for the family, particularly Matthew. I can just about cope with the actual physical endurance of my tummy being sore. That is at least contained in one place. But I loathe to see the rippling effect out to others, and especially to one whom I love so dearly. It changes our relationship—a relationship which was so very close that sometimes I feel bitter that pain could succeed in its assaults upon something so precious. Until 1980 we had never had any cross words or accusations against one another. Never.

But now we do. As always, it's the silly little things which precipitate inordinately heated responses. Instead of our giving one another strength and encouragement to pull together against the suffering, everything somehow can so easily be turned around until we seem to be pulling against one another.

Not only do I myself feel at the end of my rope with my own pain, but Matthew also feels so with his. It's as if he can last for so long watching me suffer, feeling sympathetic and supportive toward me, before he reaches the limits of his unselfishness. Suddenly he will become aware of the cost to him and he will resent it. Not me, it. But I, watching him, feel I am to blame. The pain is mine: Could I not cope better so that he does not have to suffer as well?

The other day was a bad one in the middle of a week in which I was struggling simply to keep going. I was forcing myself around the house, trying to do the basic chores. I thought I was doing well until suddenly I heard the scraping noise of the wooden stools being kicked roughly under the breakfast bar.

"No butter!" came a heated explosion. Matthew was peeved. He likes butter on his toast in the morning; that is one of his treats to add sparkle to his "keep-fit" diet.

I cringed. I felt accused, even though he had been shouting at the situation, not at me personally. He had not known that I was just above the kitchen, slowly folding the laundry to put away. Mind you, he was sufficiently angry that he probably wouldn't have minded that I heard.

My thoughts scanned the past few days. Why was there no butter? How had I managed to let the old one run out without replacing it? I felt I had failed as Matthew's wife. A decent wife would ensure there was always enough butter for her husband's toast.

I remembered taking the empty butter dish over to the kitchen sink on the previous day. *I must get a new packet from the freezer,* I had thought wearily as I took the brush to wash it. *Later,* I added, thinking how far away the garage seemed at the moment. And later, of course, I had forgotten.

Now, as I carried the neatly folded tea towels into the kitchen, I wondered what to say. This was my fault. I could not really blame pain for such a small thing. I had been lazy, then I had forgotten.

Matthew was not there. He was bashing about in his study now. Up on the wall, my shopping list was pinned as usual to the bulletin board. Its whole page was filled with one word sprawled across it: *BUTTER*.

I felt sorry for myself as I closed the drawer on my fresh supply of tea towels. I thought of all I had done over the past week, battling against how I had felt physically. And Matthew wasn't appreciative. All he was doing this morning was shouting at what I had failed to do.

In this sense of failure, feeling overwhelmed by pain, one of the worst things I can do is look ahead. To endure patiently is much harder when there seems to be no time limit to the pain. How quickly a feeling of desperation, a sort of claustrophobia, can come.

The most tedious aspect of chronic pain is its relentlessness. I sometimes feel trapped by it. I find myself saying, *I cannot bear this.* I feel I could somehow cope if I could look forward to a day or a time when the pain will end, to console myself that I will soon feel better. Even the same afternoon can seem exhaustingly far ahead, and I feel, *I cannot get through until the children are in bed. I'll surely crack up before then.* But that is looking ahead.

Instead, I am trying to learn how to look only at the present. I should say to myself, *You ARE bearing it, Jane,* because pain is deceptive. It gives the impression that it will overwhelm me for a long time. In practice, often just one day makes a huge difference. Within a few hours, unbearable pain can change and become almost bearable. And of course, it is well known that pain is affected by morale. I am almost ashamed to confess that the most trivial accomplishments, such as washing the dishes, can lift my morale enough to make the pain seem less intolerable.

Others can and do help. Matthew and I are frequently amazed by the sacrifices made by our family and friends in order to help us, in whatever ways they choose. And yet, even that can have its own tension. People do what seems best, but that is not always what might help most.

Anyone who helps me practically represents God helping me practically. One day a friend, Annegret, phoned to ask about me. I told her I was unwell again. This time it was not so bad as to warrant admission to the hospital, but I was in a lot of pain. Within two hours she had come to the house, bringing food she had lovingly cooked for our family for the next week. She thought this was meager help in the face of such suffering — she would have preferred to take away my pain. Yet her visit to me was like a visit from God Himself saying, "This is a sign that I care about you, even in the practicalities."

However, on another occasion two people came unannounced with four meals between them. A big treat? Yes, except that all of it had previously been frozen and needed to be eaten soon. To make matters more complicated, there was already food in our refrigerator which had to be cooked before it went bad. So while outwardly thanking the caring friends for their thoughtful gifts, Matthew was inwardly groaning. He still had to cook; he still had to think how he could best use the food; he still had to plan which dish had to be cooked most immediately. And just as he closed the door on those friends, the children were bored.

The living room seemed uninviting and stale now. The glass-topped tables were smeared with grubby fingerprints. Shelves were cluttered with empty cups. Matthew dragged himself into the depressing scene, just in time to catch Philippa. Enjoying her new-found skill of crawling, she had just reached up for the brightly shining sugar bowl.

As she grabbed clumsily for it, she knocked over a half-empty cup.

"Disgusting!" muttered Matthew under his breath, stomping heavily toward her. He lifted her exploring arms from patting the cold tea, now dripping onto the carpet, and carried her through to the kitchen to wash her. There, too, he was met with a mess. Cake tins were still left out from the folk who had brought the food. He snapped one lid closed but, before he could put it away, there was a sudden wail from the living room.

Angus had become bored after enduring visitors one after another. Each had excluded him from their discussion of "important" things. At three years old he could have made his own contribution to the conversation about Mommy's sore tummy. He would have enjoyed explaining that she had had a tube in her "bud vessel," which he thought looked like a train going along a train track. But people had not expected him to converse, so he had not. Instead he had set up an obstacle course, jumping from a wooden chair onto a huge floor cushion. It had amused him for a while, until one jump when he bumped his head on the bookshelf.

Matthew raced through. Tears flowed freely—more out of boredom than physical pain. Angus wanted to let Matthew know that he wanted as much time with his daddy as others got. Grown-ups somehow had the knack of demanding attention immediately; when they rang the doorbell, Matthew answered it and there ensued a conversation. Angus seldom enjoyed the same indulgence of Matthew's undivided attention. He had come second to the doorbell and the telephone. He was still too little to have learned how to demand time sociably from Matthew's busy life, except by a huge wail.

Matthew sat cradling Angus, stroking his hair. He admired the obstacle course and soon they were both laughing about the bumped head. "Bumps are inevitable if we do dangerous things to enjoy life," they agreed. "Pain is worthwhile when we've had fun."

Upstairs in bed, I heard it all.

"Would you like a story?" Matthew suggested to Angus. Stories were a good opportunity for a quietly intimate time together. That would entertain him.

"Oooh!" came the enthusiastic reply, and Angus ran to choose a book.

But Matthew's voice did not hold the same enthusiasm now. His reading was mechanical today. His mind was not with Thomas the Tank Engine. It was in the study, thinking about his work. He needed space to think. How best could he encourage those four mothers to help with a new nursery service in church? How were the three teenagers coping whose mother died last week? What could he do to catch the interest of the children in tomorrow's school assembly? That was work—his work. Amusing children was not real work; not in the same fulfilling way. How could he do justice to God in his work this week without time? Time to think? Time to pray?

The story over, and Philippa contentedly emptying a fresh box of toys, Matthew planned how he might snatch a few moments to think on his own. He began to gather together the empty mugs. "You just carry on while I try to tidy up a bit," he suggested to Angus.

But Angus was still bored; no suggestion caught his imagination now. "May I watch television? *My* program?" he asked, recognizing the distinctive set of the clock's hands at 4 P.M. for the start of children's television.

Matthew was thwarted from carrying through with the dishes. He turned around, frustrated from his plans and irritated that Angus had succeeded in squeezing a little more of his attention. If it wasn't friends calling it was Angus, or the telephone, or Philippa. And he hadn't been upstairs to see me for a while . . . me, quietly shedding a tear after hearing their earlier conversation. "Pain is worthwhile when we've had fun," they had said. *What about when it prevents us from having fun in the first place?* I was wondering. I was glad Matthew had not come up. I would only have been yet another burden on him. He was suffering enough already.

"Well, it depends on what the TV program is," Matthew conceded reluctantly. But already Angus had raced over to press the switch. "Paddington!" he cried with glee. "Mommy lets me watch this!"

Matthew trudged through to the kitchen. He felt trampled on, taken over; as if he had no place to make decisions any more. He was ruled by the ricocheting effect of my pain.

Upstairs I could not settle. Although I was resting physically, my mind was in turmoil. I could understand some of Matthew's pain and I wanted to help. I was sorry for him, yet also afraid of his anger. I knew he might blow up at someone — maybe at the children, maybe at me. I knew it would not be meant personally if he did. Just as I sometimes have to bear more physical pain than I feel able, now he was bearing too much emotional and mental pain.

Does it seem ungrateful of Matthew to be burdened by others' help? Therein lies yet another source of tension for him. He knows he must be grateful to others for all help offered. He would hate to hurt them by suggesting that their good will could be better channeled. So he bears more — silently.

Inevitably, he feels a reaction. I want him to be free to express his reaction, and not try to suppress everything, bottling up his feelings inside himself. He's inclined to do that anyway, having been taught at boarding school that it is "good" not to show unpleasant emotions. So strongly has this been ingrained in him that he automatically feels guilty when he finds anger within himself. At that stage he either denies it or falls silent (easily mistaken for moodiness) as he tussles within himself.

On the one hand Matthew wants to weep for me and shout out against the apparent injustice that he should see me suffer more than many others; on the other hand he has this strong inbuilt sense that he should be able to cope. This is made even stronger whenever he recognizes God's hand working within all our suffering. If God is so clearly in it, then shouldn't Matthew be able to come through with a glowing Christian serenity?

In addition to this tension, he has to deal with the practical everyday chores, such as keeping the children happy and finding the next meal — things which he is unaccustomed to doing simultaneously.

One of the ways in which other people help us endure with patience is by encouraging us in every way, including in prayer. Not the insistent kind of prayer which tells God what to do, but the quiet waiting upon Him together. I was helped not only by the direct effect of prayer on myself, but also because I could see how much Matthew was strengthened and made more peaceful by it.

Every Monday for about eighteen months, while Matthew was at seminary, about a dozen faithful friends joined together to pray. They began meeting like this in 1980 while I was so critically ill, but they did not give up as soon as the crisis had passed. Even other very worthwhile demands on their time did not make them cease. For Matthew and myself, their faithfulness was an enormous encouragement. For themselves, they became convinced that those who pray benefit as much as the one being prayed for.

There was one such evening, just before Easter 1980, when the group was drawn to one particular verse which has continued to be a great source of strength. They had been silent for a long time as they simply lifted me to God in their minds. A stillness came upon them, gentle yet powerful. Then the quietness was broken by three different people.

"I have a tune repeating itself over and over in my ears," said Peter.

"I have a picture in my mind," said Anne.

"I have a verse which I cannot get out of my head," was John's contribution. "But I'm not sure where to find it."

"Maybe someone else will know?" Alastair was leading that evening. "Tell us what it is."

The words came easily as John spoke the verse: "The steadfast love of the Lord never ceases, his mercies never come to an end" (Lamentations 3:22). Little could he guess how much his trust in those words would be tested in the following years, with the long and continuing illness of his wife, Sadie.

"It's amazing that you should quote that verse!" exclaimed Peter. "Because the tune which came to me was from the song with those very words." He picked up his guitar, and everyone joined in quietly to sing the song about the Lord's steadfast love.

After it was finished, it was Anne's turn. "My picture fits in with both the verse and the song," she said. "I can see a crocus, a beautiful crocus. The outer leaves are curled around the fragile petals of the flower. It's like loving hands protecting something, or someone, very precious."

The room was silent again while everyone reflected on what had been shared. They all marvelled at the one message of assurance and love, given so clearly in three different ways, but at the same time. Gradually the hush became diffused with praise, in prayer and in song, that God's Spirit should so graciously be among them.

I had been too tired to go to this particular meeting, but as soon as Matthew returned home afterwards I could see that he had something tremendous to share. He was surrounded by an aura of peace which was somehow very positive and powerful.

The group did not share this verse with me glibly, as a quick means of explaining my pain away without entering into our suffering. The verse itself was actually written in the context of enormous suffering. It was a cry uttered by Jeremiah among shouts of anguish to the Lord: "He [God] has . . . brought me into darkness without any light" (Lamentations 3:2). Yet Jeremiah's hope returned whenever he remembered that God's steadfast love remained, even in the depths of suffering: "Though he cause grief, he will have compassion" (Lamentations 3:32).

When my own trust crumbles, and questioning turns into doubt, it is not only my physical strength which fails: I weaken emotionally and spiritually, too, and have to depend on others' help. Even though I was not there myself, that special evening gave me a profound trust in the Lord's steadfast love – no matter what. Through others waiting on God, as if on my behalf, I have been given Lamentations 3 as a special source of comfort.

In order to keep this verse meaningful to me, I must be patient. To look for a time limit is to lose patience. I have had to learn how to grit my teeth and force myself to get through. But that is not the sort of patience God wants for me – He wants me to learn patience with joy.

I remember reading the book of Colossians while feeding Philippa as a baby. Because I was then caring for the two children, time was short and I was trying to cram my prayer time and Bible reading into the brief period of peacefulness when Angus was at his playgroup. The sun streamed into our quiet living room, almost as an illustration of God's presence illumining what I was reading.

It was the first time that I had noticed the phrase "patience with joy" (Colossians 1:11). It was part of Paul's prayer for the Christians he was addressing.

"Oh, Lord," I prayed as soon as I noticed it. "I'd like patience with joy." I realized that a lot of the time my "patience" was more like long-suffering—I lacked the joy which comes from God's own patience.

"Please give me patience with joy," I prayed.

I stopped for a moment. I did not hear God's physical voice, but in the pause after my prayer a new thought came to me. It was as if God were talking.

"Patience and joy are not gifts, they are fruit—part of the fruit of the Holy Spirit. They grow, slowly but surely, like fruit on a tree. They cannot be stuck on with glue."

My momentary excitement waned a little. I realized that my prayer for patience and joy as a gift was inappropriate. If I wanted them, I had to be prepared to steep myself more fully in God's Spirit, so that He could bring forth the fruit as a natural consequence of my life in Him.

I adjusted my prayer: "Help me to live more closely to You—more *in* You than *with* You and I'll still look to You to make patience and joy grow out of my life."

I felt quite subdued as I realized what my prayer actually meant. Patience grows from endurance, endurance from suffering. To pray for patience would not mean the end of pain, but an acceptance that it could continue in order to bear fruit—God's fruit.

There would be no easy path to joy, either. To some extent joy grows out of sorrow. To ask for the fruit of the Holy Spirit to be seen in my life was to accept God's hand completely. In His great wisdom He seems to have chosen to teach me His path to joy through suffering.

It seemed, and still does seem, to be a daunting road. I only continue the apparently endless trudge of carrying on by being encouraged. I need to be affirmed that I *am* in the Lord's hands, even when it looks as if He has let go of me.

To endure with patience sounds tremendously heroic; but in reality it is tough and unexciting. Trapped in the midst of the pain, I am unable to stand back objectively in the way onlookers can. To endure patiently seems so endlessly hard; it drives one even to the point of despair.

It is paradoxical that, when I have felt like this, God has been reflected in me. I greatly value the comments of my friends to this end. Elaine's words are but one example: "Your courage and trust in the face of such suffering and ongoing discouragement cannot help but witness to the glory of God."

In the face of all I endure, this is my encouragement: I can be a light to those around me; I can please God within my suffering; I can even have a ministry in suffering.

One letter which I will always treasure is from Geoff, who came to see me when I felt particularly weary and spent. I had no idea at the time that I had anything to offer in life, to God or to others. Such knowledge would have been sufficient encouragement for me to stop feeling so low and useless. Geoff wrote:

> Thank you so much for our time together which gave me so much. It is a joy to be with you, and to see maybe something which you cannot: the quiet joy of Christ radiating through the daily painful and victorious cross that He has placed upon your frail shoulders. You may not see this "quiet joy" that I mention, but I can see it and have seen it before . . . Christ lives within you, and what we see in you is an unending limit of endurance and faithfulness which is possible only in Him.

We can be so slow in encouraging one another, yet each person who suffers desperately needs to be encouraged. He needs to know that, although much of the action in his life is completely curtailed by pain, his life is bearing fruit. It is worthwhile.

In this story you have seen how Jane Grayshon found special strength and peace by drawing on her knowledge of God's personal love for her.

If you are wondering how you can have access to the same spiritual resource, the following pages will help you. You can know, without a doubt, whether you have a right relationship with the God who created you and who loves you.

If you let Him, He will point you to your personal pathway through the pain . . . and walk with you every step of the way.

Would You Like to Know God Personally?

The following four principles will help you discover how to know God personally and experience the abundant life He promised.

1 GOD **LOVES** YOU AND CREATED YOU TO KNOW HIM PERSONALLY.

2 MAN IS **SINFUL** AND **SEPARATED** FROM GOD, SO WE CANNOT KNOW HIM PERSONALLY OR EXPERIENCE HIS LOVE.

God's Love

"For God so loved the world, that He gave His only begotten Son, that whoever believes in Him should not perish, but have eternal life" (John 3:16).

God's Plan

"Now this is eternal life: that they may know you, the only true God, and Jesus Christ, whom you have sent" (John 17:3, NIV).

What prevents us from knowing God personally?

Man Is Sinful

"For all have sinned and fall short of the glory of God" (Romans 3:23).

Man was created to have fellowship with God; but, because of his stubborn self-will, he chose to go his own independent way, and fellowship with God was broken. This self-will, characterized by an attitude of active rebellion or passive indifference, is evidence of what the Bible calls sin.

Man Is Separated

"For the wages of sin is death" (spiritual separation from God) (Romans 6:23).

This diagram illustrates that God is holy and man is sinful. A great gulf separates the two. The arrows illustrate that man is continually trying to reach God and establish a personal relationship with Him through his own efforts, such as a good life, philosophy or religion.

HOLY GOD

SINFUL MAN

The third principle explains the only way to bridge this gulf . . .

3

JESUS CHRIST IS GOD'S ONLY PROVISION FOR MAN'S SIN. THROUGH HIM ALONE WE CAN KNOW GOD PERSONALLY AND EXPERIENCE HIS LOVE.

He Died in Our Place

"But God demonstrates His own love toward us, in that while we were yet sinners, Christ died for us" (Romans 5:8).

He Rose From the Dead

"Christ died for our sins . . . He was buried . . . He was raised on the third day, according to the Scriptures . . . He appeared to Peter, then to the twelve. After that He appeared to more than five hundred" (1 Corinthians 15:3-6).

He Is the Only Way to God

"Jesus said to him, 'I am the way, and the truth, and the life; no one comes to the Father, but through Me' " (John 14:6).

This diagram illustrates that God has bridged the gulf which separates us from Him by sending His Son, Jesus Christ, to die on the cross in our place to pay the penalty for our sins.

It is not enough just to know these truths . . .

4

WE MUST INDIVIDUALLY RECEIVE JESUS CHRIST AS SAVIOR AND LORD; THEN WE CAN KNOW GOD PERSONALLY AND EXPERIENCE HIS LOVE.

We Must Receive Christ

"But as many as received Him, to them He gave the right to become children of God, even to those who believe in His name" (John 1:12).

We Receive Christ Through Faith

"For by grace you have been saved through faith; and that not of yourselves, it is the gift of God; not as a result of works, that no one should boast" (Ephesians 2:8,9).

When We Receive Christ, We Experience a New Birth. (Read John 3:1-8.)

We Receive Christ by Personal Invitation

(Christ is speaking): "Behold, I stand at the door and knock; if anyone hears My voice and opens the door, I will come in to him" (Revelation 3:20).

Receiving Christ involves turning to God from self (repentance) and trusting Christ to come into our lives to forgive our sins and to make us the kind of people He wants us to be. Just to agree intellectually that Jesus Christ is the Son of God and that He died on the cross for our sins is not enough. Nor is it enough to have an emotional experience. We receive Jesus Christ by faith, as an act of the will.

These two circles represent two kinds of lives:

SELF-DIRECTED LIFE

S — Self is on the throne

† — Christ is outside the life

● — Interests are directed by self, often resulting in discord and frustration

CHRIST-DIRECTED LIFE

† — Christ is in the life and on the throne

S — Self is yielding to Christ

● — Interests are directed by Christ, resulting in harmony with God's plan

Which circle best represents your life? Which circle would you like to have represent your life?

The following explains how you can invite Jesus Christ into your life . . .

YOU CAN RECEIVE CHRIST RIGHT NOW BY FAITH THROUGH PRAYER

(Prayer is talking with God)

God knows your heart and is not so concerned with your words as He is with the attitude of your heart. The following is a suggested prayer:

"Lord Jesus, I want to know You personally. Thank You for dying on the cross for my sins. I open the door of my life and receive You as my Savior and Lord. Thank You for forgiving my sins and giving me eternal life. Take control of the throne of my life. Make me the kind of person You want me to be."

Does this prayer express the desire of your heart?

If it does, pray this prayer right now, and Christ will come into your life, as He promised.

How to Know That Christ Is in Your Life

Did you receive Christ into your life? According to His promise in Revelation 3:20, where is Christ right now in relation to you? Christ said that He would come into your life and be your friend so you can know Him personally. Would He mislead you? On what authority do you know that God has answered your prayer? (The trustworthiness of God Himself and His Word.)

The Bible Promises Eternal Life to All Who Receive Christ

"And the witness is this, that God has given us eternal life, and this life is in His Son. He who has the Son has the life; he who does not have the Son of God does not have the life. These things I have written to you who believe in the name of the Son of God, in order that you may know that you have eternal life" (1 John 5:11-13).

Thank God often that Christ is in your life and that He will never leave you (Hebrews 13:5). You can know on the basis of His promise that Christ lives in you and that you have eternal life, from the very moment you invite Him in. He will not deceive you.

An important reminder . . .

DO NOT DEPEND ON FEELINGS

The promise of God's Word, the Bible—not our feelings—is our authority. The Christian lives by faith (trust) in the trustworthiness of God Himself and His Word. This train diagram illustrates the relationship between fact (God and His Word), faith (our trust in God and His Word), and feeling (the result of our faith and obedience) (John 14:21).

The train will run with or without the caboose. However, it would be useless to attempt to pull the train by the caboose. In the same way, we, as Christians, do not depend on feelings or emotions, but we place our faith (trust) in the trustworthiness of God and the promises of His Word.

Fellowship in a Good Church

God's Word admonishes us not to forsake "the assembling of ourselves together" (Hebrews 10:25). Several logs burn brightly together, but put one aside on the cold hearth and the fire goes out. So it is with your relationship with other Christians. If you do not belong to a church, do not wait to be invited. Take the initiative; call the pastor of a nearby church where Christ is honored and His Word is preached. Start this week, and make plans to attend regularly.

Suggestions for Christian Growth

Spiritual growth results from trusting Jesus Christ. "The righteous man shall live by faith" (Galatians 3:11). A life of faith will enable you to trust God increasingly with every detail of your life.

* * * * *

Steven L. Pogue has written an excellent book designed to help you make the most of your new life in Christ. The title is **The First Year of Your Christian Life,** and it is available in Christian bookstores everywhere, or you can call 1-800-950-4457 to order from the publisher.

Real Help
for Real Hurts

Watch for
Jane Grayshon's
inspiring sequel
to be published
July 1991

Another quality book from

Here's Life Publishers